Attention Deficits and Hyperactivity in Children

Developmental Clinical Psychology and Psychiatry Series

Series Editor: Alan E. Kazdin, Yale University

Recent volumes in this series . . .

8: LIFE EVENTS AS STRESSORS IN CHILDHOOD AND ADOLESCENCE
by James H. Johnson

9: CONDUCT DISORDERS IN CHILDHOOD AND ADOLESCENCE
by Alan E. Kazdin

10: CHILD ABUSE
by David A. Wolfe

11: PREVENTING MALADJUSTMENT FROM INFANCY THROUGH ADOLESCENCE
by Annette U. Rickel and LaRue Allen

12: TEMPERAMENT AND CHILD PSYCHOPATHOLOGY
by William T. Garrison and Felton J. Earls

14: MARRIAGE, DIVORCE, AND CHILDREN'S ADJUSTMENT
by Robert E. Emery

15: AUTISM
by Laura Schreibman

18: DELINQUENCY IN ADOLESCENCE
by Scott W. Henggeler

19: CHRONIC ILLNESS DURING CHILDHOOD AND ADOLESCENCE
by William T. Garrison and Susan McQuiston

20: ANXIETY DISORDERS IN CHILDREN
by Rachel G. Klein and Cynthia G. Last

21: CHILDREN OF BATTERED WOMEN
by Peter G. Jaffe, David A. Wolfe, and Susan Kaye Wilson

22: SUBSTANCE ABUSE IN CHILDREN AND ADOLESCENTS
by Steven P. Schinke, Gilbert J. Botvin, and Mario A. Orlandi

23: CHILD PSYCHIATRIC EPIDEMIOLOGY
by Frank C. Verhulst and Hans M. Koot

24: EATING AND GROWTH DISORDERS IN INFANTS AND CHILDREN
by Joseph L. Woolston

25: NEUROLOGICAL BASIS OF CHILDHOOD PSYCHOPATHOLOGY
by George W. Hynd and Stephen R. Hooper

26: ADOLESCENT SEXUAL BEHAVIOR AND CHILDBEARING
by Laurie Schwab Zabin and Sarah C. Hayward

27: EFFECTS OF PSYCHOTHERAPY WITH CHILDREN AND ADOLESCENTS
by John R. Weisz and Bahr Weiss

28: BEHAVIOR AND DEVELOPMENT IN FRAGILE X SYNDROME
by Elisabeth M. Dykens, Robert M. Hodapp, and James F. Leckman

29: ATTENTION DEFICITS AND HYPERACTIVITY IN CHILDREN
by Stephen P. Hinshaw

30: LEARNING DISABILITIES
by Byron P. Rourke and Jerel E. Del Dotto

Attention Deficits and Hyperactivity in Children

Stephen P. Hinshaw

Volume 29.
Developmental Clinical Psychology and Psychiatry

SAGE Publications
International Educational and Professional Publisher
Thousand Oaks   London   New Delhi

For information address:

SAGE Publications, Inc.
2455 Teller Road
Thousand Oaks, California 91320

SAGE Publications Ltd.
6 Bonhill Street
London EC2A 4PU
United Kingdom

SAGE Publications India Pvt. Ltd.
M-32 Market
Greater Kailash I
New Delhi 110 048 India

Printed in the United States of America

Library of Congress Cataloging-in-Publication Data

Hinshaw, Stephen P.
  Attention deficits and hyperactivity in children / Stephen P. Hinshaw.
        p. cm. —(Developmental clinical psychology and psychiatry: v. 29)
  Includes bibliographical references and index.
  ISBN 0-8039-5195-7. — ISBN 0-8039-5196-5 (pbk.)
  1. Attention-deficit hyperactivity disorder.   I. Title.
II. Series.
RJ506.H9H56 1994
618.92'8589—dc20   93-36735

94 95 96 97 10 9 8 7 6 5 4 3 2 1

Sage Production Editor: Diane S. Foster

CONTENTS

Series Editor's Introduction   vii

Preface   ix

1. **Background Issues, Core Symptoms, and Associated Features**   1

   Key Background Issues   3
   Defining Features   12
   Prevalence   12
   Harmful Dysfunction?   15
   Associated Features and Comorbidity   16
   Progression Into Adolescence and Adulthood   18
   Summary   19

2. **Assessment and Diagnosis**   22

   Reliability and Validity   25
   Cross-Informant Consistency in the Assessment of ADHD   28
   Theoretical Framework for Assessment   29
   Key Assessment Tools   31
   Amalgamating Disparate Sources of Information   39
   Summary   41

3. **The Nature of the Disorder and Etiologic Hypotheses**   43

   Methodologic and Conceptual Issues   44
   The Nature of ADHD: Underlying Mechanisms   45
   Etiology   57
   Summary   65

4. **Subgroups and Comorbidity**   67

   Pervasive Versus Situational Hyperactivity   67
   Attention Deficit Disorder With and Without Hyperactivity   70

Comorbid Aggression in Children With ADHD   74
Associated Learning Disabilities and Underachievement   76
Comorbid Anxiety Disorders and Depression   77
Girls With ADHD   79
Summary   81

**5. Course, Developmental Progressions,
and Predictors of Outcome   84**

Natural History of ADHD   84
Developmental Progressions and Predictors of Outcome   88
Which Factors Reliably Predict Long-Term Outcome
   in Children With ADHD?   98
Summary   99

6. Intervention Strategies   101

Conceptual Underpinnings of Treatment   103
Pharmacologic Intervention for ADHD   105
Behavioral Intervention for ADHD   112
Treatment Combinations   118
NIMH Multimodal Treatment Study
   for Children With ADHD   122
Final Thoughts   123

References   127

Index   147

About the Author   155

SERIES EDITOR'S INTRODUCTION

Interest in child and adolescent development and adjustment is by no means new. Yet only recently has the study of youth benefited from advances in both clinical and scientific research. Advances in the social and biological sciences, the emergence of disciplines and subdisciplines that focus exclusively on childhood and adolescence, and greater appreciation of the impact of such influences as the family, peers, and school have helped accelerate research on developmental psychopathology. Apart from interest in the study of child development and adjustment for its own sake, the need to address clinical problems of adulthood naturally draws one to investigate precursors in childhood and adolescence.

Within a relatively brief period, the study of psychopathology among children and adolescents has proliferated considerably. Several different professional journals, annual book series, and handbooks devoted entirely to the study of children and adolescents and their adjustment document the proliferation of work in the field. Nevertheless, there is a paucity of resource material that presents information in an authoritative, systematic, and disseminable fashion. There is a need within the field to convey the latest developments and to represent different disciplines, conceptual views, and approaches to the topics of childhood and adolescent adjustment and maladjustment.

The Sage Series *Developmental Clinical Psychology and Psychiatry* is designed to serve uniquely several needs of the field. The series encompasses individual monographs prepared by experts in the fields of clinical child psychology, child psychiatry, child development, and related disciplines. The primary focus is on *developmental psychopathology,* which in this volume refers here to the diagnosis, assessment, treatment, and prevention of problems that arise in the period from infancy through adolescence. A working assumption of the Series is that understanding, identifying, and treating problems of youth must draw on multiple disciplines and diverse views within a given discipline.

The task for individual contributors is to present the latest theory and research on various topics including specific types of dysfunction, diagnostic and treatment approaches, and special problem areas that affect adjustment. Core topics within clinical work are addressed by the series. Authors are asked to bridge potential theory, research, and clinical practice and to outline the current status and future directions. The goals of the series and the tasks presented to individual contributors are demanding. We have been extremely fortunate in recruiting leaders in the fields who have been able to translate their recognized scholarship and expertise into highly readable works on contemporary topics.

The present monograph, prepared by Dr. Stephen Hinshaw, focuses on attention deficits and hyperactivity in children. The topic has received a great deal of attention in research and is commonly encountered by parents, teachers, and therapists in everyday life. In many ways, attention deficits and hyperactivity serve as a showcase for many advances as well as challenges before researchers and practitioners in the mental health professions. In this book, Dr. Hinshaw masterfully presents advances and challenges in diverse areas including diagnosis, assessment, etiology, and intervention. The developmental course of the attention deficits is traced, with an effort to identify promising and needed interventions to improve current practice. The book is enriched by the fact that the author's own work has played an important role in elaborating key features of attention deficits. Overall, the monograph provides a comprehensive yet concise presentation of attention deficits, current advances, and sources of controversy that currently guide both clinical research and practice.

Alan E. Kazdin, Ph.D.

PREFACE

The amount of literature that has been published in recent years regarding the constellation of behavioral and cognitive problems commonly known as hyperactivity, attention deficit disorder, or attention-deficit hyperactivity disorder (ADHD) is nothing short of staggering. Supplementing the countless journal articles that appear each year, a number of books on the topic have appeared within the past decade, including a provocative monograph (Conners & Wells, 1986) in this very series on *Developmental Clinical Psychology and Psychiatry.* Attempting to synthesize findings from this vast and often confusing array of information is both daunting and challenging.

Furthermore, misinformation abounds in the field. Public and even professional understanding of children with clinically significant attention problems and overactivity is limited by outdated notions, suboptimal assessment strategies, nonreplicated scientific findings, and pervasive tendencies to pursue narrow, unidimensional perspectives in both scholarship and intervention. Regarding the latter point, such prior terms as minimal brain dysfunction for many years ascribed causation exclusively to neural mechanisms, whereas other paradigms looked solely toward deviant parent-child interaction as the key etiologic factor. Notions of complex causal pathways in which psychobiologic risk factors, problematic family functioning, and wider system influences might combine to shape problems in attention regulation, activity level modulation, and response inhibition have been slow to gain acceptance.

My chief goals for this book are as follows: (a) to provide sufficient background information regarding basic clinical, conceptual, diagnostic, etiologic, and treatment-related issues so that readers are conversant with major themes; and (b) to illuminate and critically evaluate several key debates and core questions that have confronted the field for many years and that still merit close consideration. Such questions include the following: Is there a valid syndrome characterized by attentional deficits and/or hyperactivity? What tools can assessors utilize to gain optimal information about the problems under consideration? Has the field achieved any consensus with respect to the nature or underlying mechanisms of the behavioral difficulties these children display? Have specific etiologic conditions been discovered? Do valid subtypes of hyperactive children exist? Which factors predict subsequent functioning in adolescence or adulthood? Is there continuity between treatment processes that produce short-term gains for these children and those needed to promote long-term amelioration? My intention is not to provide exhaustive coverage of all pertinent issues and controversies in the field. Indeed, far more pages than those in a slender monograph would be required to perform such a task. (For richly detailed, thorough expositions of a great many topics related to attentional deficits and hyperactivity, the reader is referred to the comprehensive books of Ross and Ross, 1982, and Barkley, 1990.) Overall, I hope to provide heuristic perspectives as well as a critical review of key issues.

Because of the great diversity of both characteristic features and causal influences related to ADHD, I consider a wide array of perspectives in synthesizing the current literature, including clinical, developmental, psychodiagnostic, psychobiologic, environmental/familial, and social cognitive viewpoints. Increasingly, scholars in the field must be well versed in a broad range of disciplines and subdisciplines. Also, because I believe that clarification of theoretical and methodologic issues is essential to understand the phenomena of interest, I periodically pause to provide illumination of relevant concepts. As well, I should state at the outset my firm belief that investigators of this childhood condition can integrate basic and applied research goals. With proper designs, intervention-related studies can inform the field with respect to underlying mechanisms; and breakthroughs in treatment await clearer understanding of fundamental biological, familial, and psychological processes.

My hope is that this book will stimulate students, trainees, and professionals in psychology, psychiatry, education, and related fields to pursue integrated clinical and scholarly aims with respect to children displaying these troublesome and distressingly persistent problems. It must be kept in mind that the sciences of clinical child psychology, developmental psychopathology, and child psychiatry are still quite young; the field has far to go before definitive answers about attention deficits and hyperactivity are forthcoming.

I deeply appreciate the invitation to prepare this monograph offered by series editor Alan Kazdin, whose incisive comments and wry humor have been, as always, quite welcome. I have also benefited greatly, over the years, from discussions and exchanges with a number of colleagues, particularly Howard Abikoff, Cari Anderson, Estol Carte, Drew Erhardt, Jonathan Fleischacker, Tracy Heller, Barbara Henker, Cheryl Herbsman, Katherine Leddick, Jamie McHale, Sharon Melnick, Rich Milich, Joel Nigg, Teron Park, Bill Pelham, John Richters, Cassandra Simmel, Jim Swanson, Carol Whalen, and Brian Zupan. Finally, I have learned enormously from the many children and families who have participated in the summer research projects and treatment programs—supported by National Institute of Mental Health grants 45064 and 50461—that I have conducted. It is to these youngsters and their parents that this book is dedicated.

1

BACKGROUND ISSUES, CORE SYMPTOMS, AND ASSOCIATED FEATURES

Children who display extreme levels of attention deficits and hyperactivity have been noticed—and undoubtedly bemoaned and stigmatized—for centuries. Yet only since the advent of compulsory education, which mandates self-controlled behavior in large-group settings, have children with such difficulties emerged in sufficient numbers to receive systematic inquiry. In recent decades, these youngsters have been among the most frequently referred for clinical services. As the field has increasingly recognized the many current and long-term difficulties faced by such children, research efforts have dramatically escalated.

Beyond their core problems in attention regulation, activity level modulation, and impulsivity, children who today receive the diagnosis of attention-deficit hyperactivity disorder (ADHD) are hindered in key domains that are of central importance for development. Specifically, they often have major difficulties with achievement in school, whether or not they display formal learning disabilities; they frequently exhibit defiance, aggression, and other antisocial behaviors; and they are nearly uniformly rejected by peers. Each of these domains is clearly associated with a negative prognosis (Huesmann, Eron, Lefkowitz, & Walder, 1984; Parker & Asher, 1987; Spreen, 1988). Understanding the linkages between, on the one hand, regulation of attention and activity level and, on the other, major developmental difficulties in learning, aggression control, and social relationships is a major goal for the field (see Chapter 3).

Despite (a) the plethora of diagnostic labels that have been used over the years to describe children with problems in the domains of attention and overactivity, (b) the heterogeneity of such children's presenting

1

difficulties, and (c) the markedly divergent paradigms and perspectives employed by different investigators in the field, several key points are clearly established. First, meaningful problems in the domains under consideration plague a sizable number of school-aged children, with prevalence estimates of formal diagnostic categories ranging from 1% to 7% (American Psychiatric Association, 1987; Anderson, Williams, McGee, & Silva, 1987; Bird et al., 1988; Schachar, 1991; Szatmari, Offord, & Boyle, 1989). Second, such problems are not limited to Western, industrialized societies but appear in diverse cultures (e.g., Bhatia, Nigam, Bohra, & Malik, 1991). Third, ADHD comprises a major public health problem with respect to both physical and psychological well-being. For example, diagnosed youngsters are at increased risk for accidents and poisonings, probably related to their poor judgment and increased impulsivity (Szatmari, Offord, & Boyle, 1989); in addition, developmental difficulties and discordant family relationships are widespread (Barkley, 1990). A disorder so closely linked with these types of impairing features requires systematic investigation.

Fourth, long-term adjustment difficulties are in store for a high percentage of children with ADHD. Prior notions of a benign course (Laufer & Denhoff, 1957) have been abandoned in light of well-conducted prospective follow-up studies (see review of Klein & Mannuzza, 1991), which indicate considerable risk for negative outcomes (see Chapter 5 for details). Fifth, and critically, although large-scale multisite intervention efforts are in active development (Richters et al., 1993), to date no clinically sufficient treatment strategies exist for altering the course of children with these problem constellations (Pelham & Hinshaw, 1992; Weiss & Hechtman, 1986). The challenges confronting scientists and practitioners who deal with attentional deficits and hyperactivity are indeed striking.

As noted in the Preface, my goal in this book is to present an overview of key issues regarding the assessment, diagnosis, etiology, prognosis, and treatment of children with ADHD while examining critically several longstanding debates in the field. I aim, as well, to convey a feel for the complexity of the causal pathways that may precipitate these problem domains as well as the conceptual and practical challenges facing investigators and practitioners who wish to provide meaningful intervention. At the outset, I can make only one prediction with certainty: Given the multiplicity of clinical concerns, conceptual debates, and scientific perspectives that pertain to these problems of childhood, the reader will leave these pages with more lingering questions than definitive answers.

KEY BACKGROUND ISSUES

Several background issues deserve coverage. These include the question of which perspective on deviance is optimal for understanding these problems, whether dimensions or categories provide the most information to scientists and practitioners, and how scientific notions of attention problems and hyperactivity have evolved over the past century. The historical review is presented to foster appreciation of the diversity of both terminology and underlying frameworks related to the domains under consideration.

Perspectives on Behavioral Deviance in Childhood

It is puzzling when a child of at least average intellectual ability constantly disrupts class, fails to stop speaking of his or her latest ideas even when it is clear that the audience is ready to move on, sings and makes noises while others are attempting to work quietly, chronically loses needed objects, insists on playing games by his or her own idiosyncratic rules, and performs erratically without ever quite seeming to reach his or her underlying potential. Why is performance so inconsistent? Can't the boundless energy and exuberant spark that are, at times, so delightful and adaptive be channeled towards productive goals rather than escalating into verbal and even physical battles? Why shouldn't the routines that have been practiced over the years be followed without exhausting prompts and reminders from parents and teachers? Although the transitory display of any of these difficulties is widespread in childhood—and although other childhood disorders include several of the core symptoms—by the time that the demands of elementary school are in place (and often as early as toddlerhood or the preschool years), perhaps 1 in 30 children displays levels of these primary problems that are noteworthy, persistent, and impairing. How are we to understand the extreme nature and lasting course of the problematic behaviors of this group of youngsters?

Biomedical Frameworks and Beyond. Can we understand such problems in the context of a medical conception of disorder or disease?[1] In our society, scientific and medical world views provide the pervasive frameworks for viewing health problems and, increasingly, emotional or behavioral concerns. At a basic level, medical models identify symptoms—in the example of ADHD, behavioral or emotional problems reported chiefly by adults—and signs, which are indicators yielded from medical examination. Syndromes are defined as clusters of co-occurring symptoms and signs; at the ultimate level, a disorder is inferred if a characteristic pathogenic process is found to underlie a syndrome. Assessment is the process of uncovering the symptom patterns of importance, and diagnosis involves the classification of the syndrome or underlying disorder into a taxonomy of disease states, known as a nosology.

Further examination of this perspective may be heuristic. First, because isolated problems of attention deficits and hyperactivity at home or in the classroom are widespread, it is difficult to know if they are "symptomatic" of underlying disorders or simply indicative of normal developmental processes. Young children (particularly boys) regularly show difficulties in attention regulation and inhibition of motoric responses, as any visit to a preschool or an early elementary school class will demonstrate (Campbell, 1990). Even with severe levels of these problems in certain children, it is often the case that environmental factors (e.g., faulty classrooms) or stressors in children's lives (a family move, parental discord) are operative. In short, symptoms of inattention, impulsivity, and overactivity in children are ubiquitous and often transitory, signifying a wide range of normal developmental processes and causal influences. The presence of (a) multiple behaviors of this type, (b) extreme deviance from developmental norms, (c) persistence over time and across situations, and (d) meaningful impairment to the child and family must be demonstrated before we can even begin to invoke notions of an underlying disorder.

Do the behavior patterns under discussion cluster together to yield a valid syndrome? Recent factor analytic investigations have converged on the finding that two dimensions or syndromes emerge when these behaviors are examined, one marked by inattention, poor concentration, restlessness, and disorganization, and the other delineated by impulse control difficulties and marked overactivity (for details, see Chapter 3). Importantly, both of these factors are distinct from dimensions marked by interpersonal aggression and frank antisocial behavior.[2] Yet when all such dimensions are themselves factor analyzed, a broad-band dimension termed *undercontrolled* or *externalizing* emerges (Achenbach & Edelbrock, 1978; Hinshaw, 1987b). Thus disinhibited behaviors and antisocial activities tend to covary.

Just as a given symptom may be quite nonspecific (e.g., fever in medicine cuts across many diseases or disorders, as does anxiety in psychopathology), syndromes themselves may not inevitably signify a uniform underlying pathology. For example, many disparate factors can trigger the syndrome of psychosis—encompassing the symptoms of loss of contact with reality, agitation, fixed false beliefs (delusions), and aberrant perceptual experiences (hallucinations)—including schizophrenia, mania, depression, overdosing of certain medications or drugs, high fever, head trauma, or viruses infecting the brain. In child psychopathology, it is similarly possible that syndromes of attention deficits-disorganization or of impulsivity/hyperactivity can each emerge from disparate underlying factors (see Chapter 3). A key goal is to discern whether at least some forms of attention deficits and hyperactivity form actual disorders, signified by a uniform cause or set of causes. Would identification of disorders be helpful?

To invoke a medical example, the syndrome constituting fever, throat infection, and lymphatic system involvement may, in some cases, relate to infection with a strain of streptococcal bacteria. The course of such bacterial infections is often far more pernicious than that triggered by viruses; in addition, intervention with antibiotics—which specifically attack the causal bacterial agents—is indicated from the diagnosis. In psychiatry and psychopathology, where known pathogenic agents are vanishingly rare (and where an infectious disease model is rarely applicable), the field often infers the presence of a disorder on the basis of such criteria as separable family historical factors, biological markers, psychological or behavioral correlates, long-term course, and treatment response for the syndrome in question. For example, the acute psychosis of a young adult may be linked to an advanced stage of mania rather than to schizophrenia, with the implications that separate genetic transmission is operative, that long-term course will be episodic or cyclic, and that a specific treatment agent (lithium carbonate) is the maintenance treatment of choice (Goodwin & Jamison, 1990).

However, for a large number of important medical syndromes, including coronary artery disease or various forms of cancer, a uniform underlying causal agent may not be detectable. In fact, disease states are increasingly believed to emanate from a constellation of risk factors and vulnerabilities in the individual, which interact with environmental threats or risks. Whereas some cancers have genetic predispositions, others may be elicited by environmental toxins or hazards; in many cases, the two types of causal factors may interact to yield disease. As our perspectives on causation must widen to consider premorbid personal functioning, environmental variables, and other risk factors that interact to create the condition, our conceptions of the nature of "disorders" must necessarily broaden as well.

From another perspective, emerging conceptions from the discipline of developmental psychopathology—in which disruptions in normal developmental patterns are held to be central to understanding aberrant behavior patterns (Sroufe & Rutter, 1984)—appear to be at considerable odds with the rather static medical-model view that deviant childhood behavior patterns form psychopathologic categories (see Cicchetti & Richters, 1993). The developmental perspective seeks processes and mechanisms of continuity and change that can account for problematic behavior, a perspective that appears diametrically opposed to the categorization of discrete illnesses or disorders characterizing the psychiatric model. In recent years, however, developmental perspectives and medical-model views of psychopathology have been at least partially bridged. Developmental viewpoints have expanded to incorporate such biological influences as temperament and genetic causation (Plomin, Nitz, & Rowe, 1990; Rutter et al., 1990b), and developmental psychopathologists are actively considering the viability of classification efforts that incorporate developmental processes (Hinshaw, Lahey, & Hart, 1993; Richters & Cicchetti, 1993). Current conceptions of the medical model include far more integrated consideration of environmental and developmental factors in shaping disordered functioning than do traditional disease-oriented perspectives characterized above. Etiologic models involving active transaction across biologic, cognitive, familial, and social/environmental levels are likely to yield greater explanatory power for the genesis and progression of attention deficits, hyperactivity, and associated aggression than are static disease-entity notions (see Moffitt, 1990; Ohman & Magnusson, 1987).

Dimensions or Categories?

In the preceding pages, I have alternated between two perspectives on attention deficits and hyperactivity. At times I have referred to a narrow-band dimension or syndrome of child dysfunction and on other occasions to a category of children who may share an underlying disorder. A contentious debate across the field of psychopathology involves just this issue: Does the appropriate subject matter pertain to dimensions of problematic functioning, or should we instead form groups of individuals with similar features? Although more thorough discussion of this core issue is found elsewhere (e.g., Eysenck, 1986), several threads of the debate bear mention.

First, inattention, hyperactivity, and impulsivity are typically assessed quantitatively, using measures such as parent or teacher rating scales, interviews with adult informants, laboratory indices of pertinent constructs, or direct behavior observations (see Chapter 2). Unless there are true discontinuities with the rest of the distribution, it may be unwise to categorize extreme scores into a "disordered" class. For one thing, statistical power is usually lost with binary, as opposed to continuous, variables; for another, the choice of cutoff points to define normal versus dysfunctional groups may well be arbitrary.

On the other hand, the typical psychiatric procedure is to establish subgroups of individuals displaying extreme profiles of behavioral or emotional functioning. Sophisticated multivariate statistical models can also be applied to ascertain the presence of discrete categories or taxa (Meehl & Golden, 1982). Such categories, it is hoped, yield disorders in the sense described earlier: A common family history, pathogenesis, and long-term course, as well as a similar treatment response, should characterize these individuals. The underlying assumption is that disordered individuals differ qualitatively from those who do not display extremes of the features.

Two pertinent examples from other areas of child psychopathology yield conflicting findings regarding the superiority of dimensions versus categories. First, for many years individuals with markedly subaverage intelligence levels (IQ scores below 45) have been classified as severely or profoundly retarded. Because the distribution of IQ scores is continuous, forming a normal curve, this cutoff might appear arbitrary, selecting individuals who simply differ in degree of intellectual functioning from moderately or mildly retarded persons. Yet the severe/profound group is, for the most part, qualitatively distinct: They display a greater prevalence than would be predicted from a strictly normal distribution, and known genetic defects serve as primary causal agents (Rutter et al., 1990a). In this case, applying a cutoff score to a continuous distribution yields a category that appears discontinuous with the remainder of the distribution.

On the other hand, Robins and McEvoy (1990) considered the dimensional versus categorical status of childhood conduct disorder (CD), which constitutes the significant display of both overt (bullying, fighting, defiance) and covert (stealing, lying, truancy, substance abuse) antisocial behaviors. In this provocative investigation, adolescent and young adult substance abuse was predicted from retrospectively recalled symptoms of childhood CD, by adults participating in the Epidemiological Catchment Area study (Robins & Regier, 1991). The question was whether substance abuse patterns would be best predicted from (a) the categorization into CD versus non-CD status or from (b) a continuous, dimensional score of the number of childhood CD symptoms. In brief, the number of child symptoms reported by the subjects made a linear, incremental prediction; each subsequent number of childhood conduct problems regularly increased the prediction of substance abuse, with no "jump" in predictive power when the threshold for a diagnosis of CD was crossed. In this instance, the dimensional perspective outperformed a categorical approach.

Unless categories are validated, with demonstrable discontinuities revealed for classified individuals versus those with subthreshold scores, the only advantages to categorical approaches would appear to be parsimony and the following of psychiatric tradition (see Hinshaw et al., 1993). Yet, as is the case for marked levels of retardation, failing to recognize actual underlying classes or diagnoses may mask significantly different developmental processes.[3] Furthermore, as demonstrated by McConaughy, Achenbach, and Kent (1988), categories of child psychopathology defined by groups with similar profiles across multiple domains of dysfunction may well outperform simple dimensions of deviant behavior. In other words, the cluster of children who display aggression as well as depression may differ qualitatively from those with similar levels of aggression but without the concomitant depression; a strategy that simply correlates aggression scores with outside criterion variables will lose this essential information. The appropriateness of dimensional versus categorical perspectives on attention deficits and hyperactivity will continue to be a key theme for the field.

Historical Conceptions

Since the turn of the century, a host of biomedical and psychosocial perspectives have been invoked to account for the troublesome behaviors under discussion.[4] This section will present only the bare essentials of historical progressions of the field's thinking, with the goal of informing the reader about the many different terms that have been used over the years and the underlying assumptions of various scientific efforts. Conceptions have swung from exclusively biomedical to exclusively psychosocial throughout much of the 20th century; only in recent decades has serious research consideration been given to more integrated, transactional models.

Over 90 years ago George Still (1902) wrote influentially about what he termed problems in "moral control" among a number of (chiefly male) child cases in the United Kingdom, most of whom did not display obvious intellectual deficits. He believed that child-rearing practices were not the usual culprit for such children's disinhibition or oppositional behavior; rather, inherited or constitutional factors were suspected as causal agents. Such notions set the stage for a host of subsequent models positing subtle brain insult as the primary cause of overly active, disinhibited, and aggressive behavior in the absence of clear intellectual retardation.

In the period during and after World War I, a worldwide epidemic of influenza and encephalitis occurred, with many survivors displaying learning problems, impulsivity, concentration difficulties, poor judgment, aggression, and overactivity, often in severe degrees. Because, in such instances, a known brain insult had led to characteristic behavioral manifestations, inferences began to be made in the other direction (Cantwell & Hanna, 1989). That is, clinical levels of disinhibition, aggression, and learning problems were attributed to underlying but undetected brain damage (see, in particular, Strauss & Lehtinen, 1947). As discussed by Barkley (1990), a host of newly discovered biological causal agents of behavioral difficulties were brought to bear in forming the argument, including birth trauma, other infectious diseases, and various types of environmental toxicity. In most instances, however, the brain damage of a wide range of dyscontrolled children was presumed rather than observed. When the unsubstantiated nature of the claim of underlying brain damage became questioned, the diagnostic label became softened to minimal brain damage and, later, minimal brain dysfunction (MBD).

Exemplifying how broad the notion of MBD had become, the work of Clements (1966) listed 99 characteristic symptoms—including problems that would currently span diagnoses ranging from learning disabilities, depression, conduct disorder, attention deficit disorders, and neurological conditions. Both the elasticity of this category and its explicit and unsubstantiated positing of underlying brain dysfunction led to its eventual demise (see Rie & Rie, 1980; Rutter, 1982). Yet intensive psychobiologic research continues to this day, with the hope of ascertaining demonstrable deficits in brain functioning for at least certain subgroups of individuals with attention deficits and hyperactivity (Zametkin et al., 1990).

Coincident with the rise of the brain damage/brain dysfunction model in the 1920s through 1940s, the child guidance movement took hold as the paradigmatic service delivery model for youth and families in the United States. The underlying theoretical base in the child guidance centers was psychoanalytic and, later, more broadly psychodynamic. Behavioral problems displayed by children were viewed as symbolic manifestations of unresolved conflict, often emanating from early caregiver-child interactions. Thus for the plurality if not the majority of children seen as outpatients during this and subsequent eras—continuing, in many parts of the country, to present times—the locus of children's attentional and behavioral problems has been attributed to largely unconscious processes, requiring play therapy techniques along with collateral therapy with the parents. It would be hard to imagine, in many respects, two more disparate theoretical models than the organic versus the psychodynamic for explaining the underlying mechanisms of attention deficits and hyperactivity.[5]

Partly in response to the broad and overstated nature of both the organic and the psychodynamic models, investigators in the 1950s and 1960s described narrower behavioral syndromes with hyperkinetic or hyperactive behavior as the central feature. Many such views were also quite organic in origin, but with greater neurologic specificity than earlier notions (e.g., Laufer & Denhoff, 1957). By 1968, the second edition of the American Psychiatric Association's *Diagnostic and Statistical Manual of Mental Disorders* described "hyperkinetic reaction of childhood" as a major category of disorders for youth (American Psychiatric Association, 1968). In the British tradition, so-called hyperkinetic behavior was also viewed as central, but diagnoses were made only in rare cases of severe and pervasive hyperkinesis, usually accompanied by major cognitive deficits. Such British conceptions, reflected in the *International Classification of Diseases* (World Health Organization, 1978), have emphasized narrower conceptions of hyperkinetic behavior (Prendergast et al., 1988).

Seminal research in Canada by Virginia Douglas led the field to the belief that the core problems of hyperkinetic or hyperactive children lay in difficulties with sustained attention, impulse control, and arousal modulation rather than in high activity level per se (see Douglas, 1983). Along with other corroborating research, this influential view led, in 1980, to a change in nomenclature within the *Diagnostic and Statistical*

Manual of Mental Disorders, Third Edition (*DSM-III*; American Psychiatric Association, 1980): The diagnosis of attention deficit disorder was characterized by developmental extremes of inattention and impulsivity, with hyperactivity itself considered secondary. Thus attention deficit disorder could exist with or without accompanying hyperactivity, yielding a fundamental dichotomy (see Chapter 4). In the *Third Edition, Revised* (*DSM-III-R*; American Psychiatric Association, 1987), terminology again changed. Attention-deficit hyperactivity disorder (ADHD) was characterized by a polythetic list of symptoms of inattention, impulsivity, and hyperactivity; subtyping on the basis of hyperactivity was essentially dropped.

During the 1980s, investigations with sophisticated methodology gave credence to the contention that overactivity itself was a primary feature for many of these children (Porrino et al., 1983). On the basis of factor analytic investigations that distinguish attention deficits and disorganization from behavioral impulsivity/hyperactivity as two fundamentally distinct dimensions (e.g., Lahey, Pelham, et al., 1988), the new *Diagnostic and Statistical Manual of Mental Disorders, Fourth Edition* (American Psychiatric Association, 1994) includes these two symptom patterns as subtypes of ADHD (see below).

The descriptive rather than explicitly etiologic nature of recent nosologies, along with their increased rigor and their operationalization of diagnostic criteria, reflects the influence of the neo-Kraepelinian movement in the United States over the last 20 years (Blashfield, 1984). Careful assessment and diagnosis are deemed critical to the success of research and clinical endeavors. Furthermore, the ascendancy of behavioral/social learning models as opposed to psychodynamic formulations is quite apparent in recent conceptions of etiology and intervention for the field (e.g., Pelham & Hinshaw, 1992). Yet psychodynamic formulations have received renewed interest with regard to the origins of attention deficits and hyperactivity: Recent longitudinal data provide evidence regarding the primacy of early caregiver-child interactions, rather than organic factors, in fostering subsequent attention deficit syndromes among high-risk, impoverished families (Jacobvitz & Sroufe, 1987). It is quite possible that differing etiologic paths lead to similar phenotypic manifestations in different subgroups of children, exemplifying the concept of equifinality (see Cicchetti & Richters, 1993). Despite markedly different underlying paradigms and assumptions, convergence among psychobiologic, social learning, and psychodynamic approaches is beginning to emerge.

In sum, the rapid changes in nomenclature and the clearly distinct underlying theories and perspectives regarding attention deficits and hyperactivity have led, at times, to a chaotic feel to the field. Yet despite variations in points of emphasis, descriptions of the constituent behaviors have been remarkably consistent over the past century, and recent etiologic formulations appear more integrative. I continue to address issues regarding the essential nature and possible etiologies of childhood attention deficits and hyperactivity in Chapter 3.

DEFINING FEATURES

As noted earlier, the predominant perspective in today's psychiatric community is that categories of disordered behavior exist. Table 1.1 lists the *DSM-IV* criteria for attention-deficit hyperactivity disorder. Such criteria reflect a considerable body of past research as well as specific investigations performed in field trials held specifically to develop the nosology. As can be seen, two parallel symptom lists emphasize, respectively, symptoms of inattention, poor concentration, and disorganization versus features related to hyperactivity and behavioral impulsivity. The diagnosis of ADHD can thus reflect a predominantly inattentive type, a hyperactive-impulsive type, or a combined type (see discussion of subtypes in Chapter 4).[6] Note that the symptoms must be developmentally extreme relative to the child's age and gender and that they must have persisted for at least 6 months, with onset before 7 years of age. In addition, the symptoms must lead to clear impairment in key domains (school, home, peer group). Furthermore, in a departure from prior American diagnostic criteria, it is required that the symptomatology be pervasive (i.e., constituent behaviors must appear at school and home). The intention is to formulate a rather restrictive set of diagnostic criteria, yielding a diagnosis that reflects clear impairment (Schachar, 1991; see also Wilson, 1993). The core features of inattention, impulsivity, and overactivity all comprise complex, multifaceted processes, extended discussion of which will occur in Chapter 3.

PREVALENCE

Prevalence estimates for a given diagnostic category reflect the stringency of the definitional criteria. Thus when adult informant rating scales are applied to nonselected populations of children (e.g., teacher

TABLE 1.1 *DSM-IV Criteria for Attention Deficit/ Hyperactivity Disorder*

A(1) Inattention: At least six of the following symptoms of inattention have persisted for at least 6 months to a degree that is maladaptive and inconsistent with developmental level:
  - (a) often fails to give close attention to details or makes careless mistakes in schoolwork, work, or other activities
  - (b) often has difficulty sustaining attenion in tasks or play activities
  - (c) often does not seem to listen to what is being said to him or her
  - (d) often does not follow through on instructions and fails to finish schoolwork, chores, or duties in the workplace (not due to oppositional behavior or failure to understand instructions)
  - (e) often has difficulty organizing tasks and activities
  - (f) often avoids or expresses reluctance about, or has difficulties in engaging in tasks that require sustained mental effort (such as schoolwork or homework)
  - (g) often loses things necessary for tasks or activities (e.g., school assignments, pencils, books, tools, or toys)
  - (h) is often easily distracted by extraneous stimuli
  - (i) often forgetful in daily activities

A(2) Hyperactivity-Impulsivity: At least 5 of the following symptoms of hyperactivity-impulsivity have persisted for at least 5 months to a degree that is maladaptive and inconsistent with developmental level:

Hyperactivity

  - (a) often fidgets with hands or feet or squirms in seat
  - (b) leaves seat in classroom or in other situations in which remaining seated is expected
  - (c) often runs about or climbs excessively in situations where it is inappropriate (in adolescents or adults, may be limited to subjective feelings of restlessness)
  - (d) often has difficulty playing or engaging in leisure activities quietly
  - (e) is always "on the go" and acts as if "driven by a motor"
  - (f) often talks excessively

Impulsivity

  - (g) often blurts out answers to questions before the questions have been completed
  - (h) often has difficulty waiting in lines or awaiting turn in games or group situations
  - (i) often interrupts or intrudes on others (e.g., butts into others' conversations or games)

B. Some symptoms that cause impairment were present before age 7.

C. Some symptoms that cause impairment must be present in two or more settings (e.g., at school, work, and at home).

D. There must be clear evidence of clinically significant impairment in social, academic, or occupational functioning.

E. Does not occur exclusively during the course of a Pervasive Developmental Disorder, Schizophrenia, or other Psychotic Disorder and is not better accounted for by a Mood Disorder, Anxiety Disorder, Dissociative Disorder, or a Personality Disorder.

TABLE 1.1 *DSM-IV Criteria for Attention Deficit/Hyperactivity Disorder*
(Continued)

Attention-Deficit/Hyperactivity Disorder, Predominantly Inattentive Type: If criterion A(1) is met but not criterion A(2) for the past 6 months.

Attention-Deficit/Hyperactivity Disorder, Predominantly Hyperactive/Impulsive Type: If criterion A(2) is met but not criterion A(1) for the past 6 months.

Attention-Deficit/Hyperactivity Disorder, Combined Type: If both criteria—A(1) and A(2)—are met for the past 6 months.

SOURCE: American Psychiatric Association. (1994). *Diagnostic and statistical manual of mental disorders* (4th ed.). Washington, DC: American Psychiatric Press. Reprinted by permission.

ratings in schools), different cutoff points will yield from 1% to 20% or more of schoolchildren as hyperactive or attention disordered. Because of the developmental and gender-related nature of the symptoms of ADHD, if a consistent cutoff is applied for youngsters of all ages and of both genders, younger children and boys (who typically show greater amounts of the behaviors in question) will be overrepresented, whereas older children and girls may be underrepresented. With such cross-sectional rating scales, in addition, specification of such important features as symptom duration and exclusion criteria (cognitive performance or adjunctive diagnoses) cannot be invoked, leading to overly broad samples.

If more stringent diagnostic criteria are employed, prevalence estimates for attention deficit disorder or ADHD in grade-school-aged children are typically in single digits. For instance, in Ontario, Canada, 9% of boys and 2% of girls met *DSM-III* criteria for attention deficit disorder (Szatmari, Offord, & Boyle, 1989). Similar figures have been found in Puerto Rico (Bird et al., 1988) and in New Zealand (Anderson et al., 1987). Note that these investigations have not insisted on so-called pervasive hyperactivity, in which prominent symptoms must be displayed both at home and school. With these more restrictive criteria of pervasiveness, prevalence rates of closer to 1% have been found (Sandoval, Lambert, & Sassone, 1980; Schachar, 1991). Prevalence estimates from unselected populations based in the United States are not currently available, although large-scale epidemiologic investigations are in the formative stages. Note that it is critically important, in epidemiologic studies, to insist on a criterion of significant impairment (as opposed to simply exhibiting a certain amount of deviant behavior) before including a child as a "case." Furthermore, the preponderance of boys with the diagnosis, most pronounced in clinic samples, is not as strong in representative community populations (e.g., Szatmari, Offord,

& Boyle, 1989). In short, earlier prevalence estimates of hyperactivity or ADHD of nearly 20% appear grossly inflated; depending on particular criteria, a range from 1% to 7% of the child population may be categorized.

HARMFUL DYSFUNCTION?

In the current nosologies, syndromes characterized by attention deficits and hyperactivity have attained the status of "mental disorders," meaning that they are rare statistically and that they cause substantial impairment to the individual and/or significant others in the environment (American Psychiatric Association, 1987). But because of the potentially deleterious effects of labeling as well as the questionable scientific validity of ascribing all deviant, problematic behavior to psychopathology, it is important to examine what criteria determine whether behavioral deviance constitutes "mental disorder." The recent perspective of Wakefield (1992) on mental disorders as harmful dysfunction is quite heuristic in this regard.

In brief, Wakefield contends that true mental disorders must (a) engender substantial harm to the individual or those around him or her and (b) incur dysfunction of natural mental mechanisms that have been selected in an evolutionary sense. Thus mere problems in living or discordant political views cannot rightly be claimed as disordered; even severely harmful behavioral patterns must reflect actual dysfunction of internal mechanisms before the status of mental disorder can be invoked. For example, the gross and pervasive distortions of cognitive and linguistic functioning linked to schizophrenia are not only extremely harmful and impairing but also yield evidence of significant dysfunction in critical mental mechanisms that are of clear value to human survival. In this sense schizophrenia would meet the "harmful dysfunction" criterion for mental disorder.

How do current conceptions of ADHD hold up under this dual criterion set? Given their association with high accident rates, severe risk for peer rejection, and negative course, there should be little doubt that clinically significant attention deficits and hyperactivity engender considerable harm. As for dysfunction, several influential conceptions of ADHD hold that the underlying deficit is one of deficient self-regulation and planful behavior (see Barkley, 1990; Douglas, 1983). It is certainly plausible that, as human brain size rapidly expanded during prehistory, the increased executive functions developing from increased self-regulatory capacities were selected for survival. In this admittedly speculative area, a child's markedly deficient self-control could therefore qualify as dysfunctional. Our ability to appraise whether mental mechanisms have been selected during the course of human evolutionary history is admittedly limited. Perhaps any set of traits favored by a given culture would be viewed as obvious products of natural selection. Nonetheless, Wakefield's conceptualization is heuristic, forcing the field to beware of reification of diagnostic categories as reflecting "mental disorders" (see Richters & Cicchetti, 1993).

ASSOCIATED FEATURES
AND COMORBIDITY[7]

As noted at the outset of this chapter, ADHD is often accompanied by the so-called secondary features of aggression, underachievement, peer rejection, and family disharmony. Yet these features are hardly secondary in importance for youngsters with ADHD. Indeed, it would be difficult to imagine a list of variables that are more predictive of maladjustment in our society than these associated aspects of the disorder.

Aggression and Antisocial Behavior

From a dimensional perspective, factors of inattention/disorganization and particularly of impulsivity/hyperactivity are at least moderately correlated with aggressive and antisocial behavior (Hinshaw, 1987b). From a categorical point of view, ADHD overlaps with CD and with oppositional-defiant disorder (ODD)—a milder form of CD featuring negative, defiant, irritable behavior patterns—at rates well above chance levels (Biederman et al., 1991). The comorbidity of ADHD with such categories ranges from 30% to 50%. In short, aggression and antisocial behavior are frequent concomitants of attention deficits and hyperactivity.

Aggression and antisocial behavior are far from unidimensional. Such subcategories as verbal versus physical aggression, instrumental versus hostile aggression, and—more globally—overt aggression versus covert antisocial behaviors are important to specify for both conceptual and clinical reasons (e.g., Loeber & Schmaling, 1985; Price & Dodge, 1989). A major problem for assessors, however, is that base rates of all aggressive and antisocial behaviors are low; detailed observational, interview, and rating methods are required to obtain a sufficient density of data to make such distinctions (see Chapter 2). Crucially, aggressive and antisocial behaviors show considerable stability throughout childhood; in fact, aggression in adulthood is quite predictable from levels of aggressive actions in middle childhood (Huesmann & Eron, 1990). Furthermore, in an investigation of youngsters with ADHD, Loney, Kramer, and Milich (1981) found that concomitant aggressive behavior was a stronger predictor of adolescent substance abuse, delinquency, and even hyperactivity than was childhood hyperactivity (see Chapter 5). In short, evaluation of aggressive and antisocial behaviors in ADHD youngsters is of extreme importance.

Academic Underachievement

The comorbidity of ADHD with formally diagnosed learning disability (LD), defined as a significant and marked discrepancy between a child's IQ and achievement scores, is lower than is often claimed, with overlap estimates ranging from 10 to 30% (Hinshaw, 1992a; Semrud-Clikeman et al., 1992). Yet the overwhelming majority of youngsters with ADHD display at least some forms of underachievement (see Fischer, Barkley, Edelbrock, & Smallish, 1990), with suboptimal academic performance exemplified by such disparate markers as the need for special education services, disruptive behavior in the classroom that interferes with learning, patterns of truancy or expulsion, grade retention, or the effects of poor sustained attention and deficient self-regulation on the mastery of school curricula. Given the central importance of school success in our society, these types of school-related difficulties are likely to be quite predictive of a negative course. In short, although overlap with formal learning disabilities is lower than often claimed, co-occurring achievement problems are a key aspect of ADHD.

Peer Rejection

The long research tradition utilizing peer sociometric assessment has consistently revealed that negative appraisal by agemates in childhood is a strong predictor of such important long-term outcomes as school dropout, delinquency, and global indices of psychopathology (Parker & Asher, 1987). Furthermore, among all categories of child behavior disorders, ADHD youngsters are among the most negatively appraised by peers (Milich & Landau, 1982; Whalen & Henker, 1992). Such peer rejection occurs over rapid time intervals: Brief videotape exposure (Bickett & Milich, 1990) or contact with a peer group for several hours (Erhardt & Hinshaw, 1993; Pelham & Bender, 1982) is sufficient to reveal stigmatization of youngsters with ADHD. Furthermore, although aggression is a potent elicitor of peer rejection (Coie, Dodge, & Kupersmidt, 1990; Erhardt & Hinshaw, 1993), nonaggressive ADHD youngsters also receive disapprobation from agemates (Pelham & Bender, 1982).[8] In all, rejection from peers is a crucial associated feature of ADHD.

Family Dysfunction

Before the field began to separate attention deficits and hyperactivity from aggression, the prevalent belief was that parents of hyperactive youngsters displayed psychopathology in the "antisocial spectrum," marked by substance abuse, delinquency, and antisocial personality in males and somatization disorders in females (Cantwell, 1975). Such features are actually concentrated only in the family members of children with aggression (alone or comorbid with ADHD); high rates of attention problems and learning problems characterize biological relatives of nonaggressive ADHD youngsters (Lahey, Piacentini, et al., 1988; Schachar & Wachsmuth, 1990). Beyond psychopathology per se, high levels of stress, a lowered sense of parenting competence, and discordant parent-child interactions are salient familial features accompanying ADHD (Anastopoulos, Guevremont, Shelton, & DuPaul, 1992; Anderson, Hinshaw, & Simmel, in press; Mash & Johnston, 1990). Although such features are rarely considered as primary causes of ADHD behavior, stressful, discordant interactions may well predict the maintenance of symptomatology and even the eventual course of the disorder (Anderson et al., in press; Campbell, March, Pierce, Ewing, & Szumowski, 1991). Furthermore, family-level problems may be a key source of intervention efforts (see Chapter 6). The family system cannot be overlooked in the evaluation of ADHD.

PROGRESSION INTO
ADOLESCENCE AND ADULTHOOD

As recently as 15 years ago it was strongly believed that hyperactivity was a benign disorder that typically disappeared with the onset of puberty. Well-conducted prospective longitudinal investigations in recent years (Barkley, Fischer, Edelbrock, & Smallish, 1990; Gittelman, Mannuzza, Shenker, & Bonagura, 1985; Mannuzza et al., 1991; Weiss & Hechtman, 1986), however, have provided strong evidence that the manifestations of ADHD often persist into adolescence and even adulthood (see review of Klein & Mannuzza, 1991). Whereas motoric hyperactivity itself may dissipate in many youngsters as they progress into adolescence, there is a strong likelihood that attentional difficulties, peer relationship problems, underachievement, and psychological sequelae will persist. Children with ADHD are at increased risk for such negative outcomes as delinquency (Satterfield, Hoppe, & Schell, 1982), early school dropout (Weiss & Hechtman, 1986), substance abuse (Gittelman et al., 1985), poor driving records (Barkley, Guevremont, Anastopoulos, DuPaul, & Shelton, 1993), and relationship difficulties (Weiss & Hechtman, 1986). Considerable variability in follow-up status exists, however, with some ADHD youths progressing to quite good outcomes, some displaying persistent social and attentional difficulties, some following an antisocial trajectory, and a few developing severe, pervasive maladjustment (Weiss & Hechtman, 1986). One clear implication is that viable intervention strategies must focus on long-range outcome goals (see Chapter 6). In Chapter 5, I examine long-term outcomes in more detail and discuss predictors of eventual course.

SUMMARY

Children with clinically significant levels of attention deficits and hyperactivity not only are bothersome to adults and noxious to peers but also tend to display developmental difficulties, family disharmony, and concurrent problems in achievement and aggression, all of which place them at strong risk for subsequent maladaptive adjustment. Whereas symptoms of inattention and overactivity are ubiquitous, syndromes marked by (a) inattention, poor concentration, and disorganization versus (b) behavioral impulsivity and overactivity appear viable. Little evidence exists, however, for uniform underlying causal agents; complex, transactional, developmental etiologies require consideration. Historic conceptions of this domain of child psychopathology have yielded swings from organic viewpoints to social learning models and psychodynamic perspectives; a wide range of identifying labels have been applied to these youngsters, leading to confusion and a slowing of scientific progress.

Currently, diagnostic criteria focus on developmentally aberrant levels of inattentive, restless, impulsive, and overactive behavior (a) that have been present since early childhood, (b) that cannot be accounted for on the basis of psychoses or pervasive developmental disorders, and (c) that are displayed in both home and school settings. Prevalence estimates have varied widely but appear to range from approximately 1% to 7%, depending on the stringency of the criteria and the requirement for cross-situational manifestations. Whether the criteria for ADHD yield evidence for "harmful dysfunction" is the topic of important debate. Importantly, ADHD is likely to incur risk for aggressive behavior, poor peer relations, underachievement, and family dysfunction; it also occurs in the presence of comorbid behavioral or emotional disorders at rates far above chance levels. The full implications of such comorbidity are only beginning to be understood. Finally, the long-term course of ADHD, though quite variable, is typically far from benign; the field is increasingly cognizant of the chronic nature of this childhood disorder. In the remainder of this book I consider assessment of both core symptomatology and associated features (Chapter 2), the nature of the disorder (Chapter 3), comorbidity and subgroups (Chapter 4), developmental trajectories and predictors of long-term outcome (Chapter 5), and perspectives on intervention (Chapter 6).

NOTES

1. Although references are commonly made to the "medical model," in actuality there are a large number of conceptions of disease and illness in medicine. Whereas the classic example is an infectious disease model, in which a specific pathogenic agent is the underlying causal factor, most modern illnesses are not infectious. As I discuss, stereotypes of biomedical perspectives must be avoided.

2. Factor analysis is a statistical technique used to ascertain underlying dimensions among a set of correlated variables. For example, among a group of 30 behavioral variables describing psychological problems of childhood, a smaller number of dimensions (for example, three) may explain a great deal of the variability among the items. The investigator then attempts to assign meaning to these dimensions of correlated variables by examining their specific content. Choices made about assessment tools and statistical procedures, however, greatly influence the number of dimensions that emerge in factor analytic studies of child psychopathology (Achenbach & Edelbrock, 1978; Hinshaw, 1987b).

3. It is conceivable, too, that the current database that we use to appraise child psychopathology—chiefly behaviors reported by adult informants—is not the optimal means of classifying disordered functioning. Perhaps underlying psychological processes, familial interaction patterns, or psychobiologic features will, in the future, yield classification into discrete groups that more accurately reflect divergent underlying categories.

4. For a detailed and richly textured accounting of historical conceptions of attention deficits and hyperactivity, the reader is strongly urged to consult Barkley (1990). Another superb historical account, with a more political perspective on the field's history, is found in Schachar (1986).

5. From another vantage point, however, the neurologic/organic and psychodynamic perspectives are quite similar in their placement of the underlying locus of the disordered

behavior inside the child. Both of these intraindividual frameworks stand in contrast to ecological views, in which features of the social environment and childhood characteristics interact to bring about deviant behavior (e.g., Whalen & Henker, 1980).

6. The *DSM-IV* hyperactive-impulsive subtype is unprecedented in past nomenclatures. Lahey (1993) has indicated that over half of the children fitting this subcategorization in the *DSM-IV* field trials were not yet in first grade, possibly indicating that the lack of exposure to a formal school curriculum had prevented the identification of inattentive-disorganized symptoms that would emerge in classroom settings.

7. When such difficulties as aggression or achievement problems are considered dimensionally, we may discuss their association or correlation with dimensions of attention deficits or hyperactivity. On the other hand, from a categorical perspective, the joint presence of two or more independent disorders in the same individual is termed cormorbidity. Importantly, ADHD more often appears in conjunction with other childhood disorders than it occurs alone (Anderson et al., 1987; Biederman, Newcorn, & Sprich, 1991). The theoretical and clinical implications of the comorbidity of ADHD with different childhood disorders are considered more fully in Chapter 4.

8. Milich and Landau (1989) point out that whereas ADHD youngsters are highly likely to be rejected by peers, and whereas ADHD-aggressive children are uniformly disliked, children with aggression alone (e.g., purely conduct-disordered youth) are sociometrically controversial, signifying their high rates of both negative and positive nominations from peers. Such a finding reinforces the importance of separating dimensions of inattention/hyperactivity from aggression in child psychopathology (Hinshaw, 1987b).

2

ASSESSMENT AND DIAGNOSIS

Evaluating children with attention deficits and hyperactivity presents challenges to traditional assessment paradigms. Before elaborating on psychometric issues, theoretical models, and preferred evaluation strategies, I discuss the nature of such challenges. First, it is necessary to realize that there is no single assessment tool that can conclusively establish a diagnosis of ADHD in a child who displays core symptoms. Rather, information from multiple sources must be weighed and synthesized, and the limitations of each informant's perspectives on attentional performance, overactivity, and poor impulse control must be taken into account. Second, because of the ubiquity of ADHD-related symptomatology across normal development and because of the frequent display of inattention and concentration difficulties in other child disorders (see Chapters 1 and 3), the assessor must obtain a careful history and must rule out differential diagnoses. Third, the usual methods for evaluating psychopathology are inadequate for the task of assessing ADHD. In the typical clinic assessment visit, the child is engaged in playroom interviews, with the play materials intended to serve as a stimulus for revealing inner thoughts, affect, and conflict. Furthermore, individual assessments of cognitive, achievement-related, and psychological functioning are typically performed; and a physician's examination will cover possible medical contributions and will often include a brief neurological examination.

These kinds of evaluations for the ADHD child, however, are quite unlikely to reflect the reports of inattention and disorganization at school as well as defiance and impulsivity at home that prompted the initial clinic contact. In fact, the majority of children with ADHD do not display the behavioral repertoire that leads to recognition by parents, teachers, and peers when they are confronted with a relatively brief one-on-one interview, clinic visit, or pediatric evaluation. In a crucial investigation performed in the early part of the last decade, Sleator and Ullmann (1981) answered the question that formed the title of their article—"Can the Physician Diagnose Hyperactivity in the Doctor's Office?"—with a resounding "no." Professionals in the field, in fact, sometimes refer to the "doctor's office effect" when a hyperactive child known for disruptive behavior at home or unfocused efforts at school presents as a model citizen during the individual attention of a clinic visit. Such behavior is not simply a facade; the novelty and one-on-one attention of a trip to the doctor's office, psychology clinic, or child guidance center are likely to elicit exemplary behavior for brief periods.

In addition, the typical "one-shot," clinic-based assessment procedure cannot capture the variability in performance that is the hallmark of ADHD (Barkley, in press). That is, such youngsters have been shown to vary widely in their performance across similar situations over time, to the considerable concern of parents, teachers, and peers. In addition to such variability, youngsters with attentional deficits and hyperactivity also appear to maintain a debilitating persistence in their behavior when situational parameters shift, in that they often fail to modulate their responses when the situation dictates change. Specifically, ADHD youngsters have been shown to persist in domineering, controlling roles even when the task demands change—for example, when shifting from teacher to learner (Whalen, Henker, Collins, McAuliffe, & Vaux, 1979) or "TV talk show host" to guest (Landau & Milich, 1988). Thus assessors must sample behavior from diverse situations over time.

Compounding the problem is that when youngsters are asked directly about their problems related to attention deficits and hyperactivity, they are prone to underreport key symptoms (Loeber, Green, Lahey, & Stouthamer-Loeber, 1991). Given the poor self-monitoring abilities of children with ADHD (Hinshaw, Henker, & Whalen, 1984a), such invalid reporting of problem behavior is not surprising.[1] The message for assessors is that whereas frank discussion with the child about problematic functioning and goal setting is necessary for treatment planning, the child's own perspective during diagnostic interviewing provides limited benefit regarding the core symptom picture of this disorder.

Overall, behavior considered hyperactive is displayed at significant levels primarily during social interactions (e.g., parent-child interchanges) or in situations emphasizing regulation and modulation of behavior (e.g., structured classroom situations; performing homework). In addition, ADHD-related behavior shows wide within-child variability over time, compounded with inflexibility in shifting roles. Adequate evaluation of this condition thus entails the repeated gathering of information from informants in the child's natural environment with regard to domains of dysfunction that are crucial for learning and social interchange. In addition to knowing the individualized evaluations of language abilities, cognitive functioning, and psychological processes that may be necessary to ensure coverage of key developmental domains, the assessor must become familiar with instruments ranging from rating scales and questionnaires to behavior observation methodologies and even peer sociometric methods, tools that provide a window on behavior and social interactions in the child's day-to-day world. The ecological validity of assessment instruments—signifying their relevance to the child's everyday ecology or environment—is not just a luxury but a necessity for the diagnosis of ADHD. In sum, assessors must capture the child's behavior in school, home, and peer-related settings and must consider the dynamic nature of symptom patterns over time and across situations.

Before proceeding with specific assessment strategies, I first review several important psychometric issues regarding assessment, with specific focus on the concepts of reliability and validity. I then discuss the important topic of whether different informants regarding child problem behavior agree with one another—a thorny issue for the field. After covering theoretical underpinnings of the assessment of attention deficits and hyperactivity, I next describe, in concise fashion, several representative assessment tools relevant to both core symptomatology and associated features. I close with discussion of issues and problems related to combining assessment information from disparate sources.

At the outset I must emphasize that because ADHD symptomatology compromises functioning in important domains related to developmental competence—most notably, academic performance, peer relationships, and family relations (see Chapter 1)—the assessor cannot simply be conversant with a handful of rating instruments or interview schedules pertinent to inattention and hyperactivity but must be widely versed in the evaluation of such critical target areas as well. In addition, because of the ubiquity of attention deficits and overactivity as symptoms that may be linked with a host of environmental stresses as well as alternative diagnostic categories (e.g., concentration problems that accompany depression or incipient thought disorder; "nervousness" that may signal anxiety as opposed to hyperactivity), priorities for assessment include wide clinical knowledge of the entire range of child psychopathology as well as strategies that can aid in differential diagnosis. Areas of the child's competence must also be explored. Because the material presented herein is necessarily condensed, the reader is invited to consult such sources as Barkley (1988), Breen and Altepeter (1990), and Hinshaw (1987a) for more thorough coverage of issues related to the assessment and diagnosis of ADHD.

RELIABILITY AND VALIDITY

Reliability

As discussed in far more detail elsewhere (Anastasi, 1988), the reliability of an assessment device refers to its consistency or freedom from unsystematic error. Several types of reliability are important to consider. First, an instrument should yield similar patterns of scores upon repeated administration over relatively brief periods of several weeks; test-retest reliability describes such temporal consistency, whereas stability typically refers to an instrument's consistency over periods of a year or more. Second, for an internally consistent instrument, each item specifically measures a given domain of functioning—for example, inattentiveness—without the confounding influence of other domains. Third, and crucially for diagnosis, an instrument such as a structured interview should yield the same diagnostic information when utilized by different clinicians; similarly, when behavior observations are performed, observers must concur with respect to the category of behavior that is noted. Such reliability is termed interdiagnostician or interobserver agreement.[2]

Several issues of importance for the assessment of ADHD are directly relevant to concerns with reliability. For one thing, when parents or teachers complete rating scales regarding the externalizing behavior (including ADHD symptoms) of their child, scores tend to fluctuate over the first few times the scales are completed. In fact, the initial completion of such scales often reveals more deviant scores than does the second administration, even in absence of intervention. This fluctuation is important both for the investigator who is gathering a research sample and for the clinician who is attempting to ascertain a child's diagnostic status; when possible, particularly for shorter scales, obtaining several repeated assessments may help to yield a more stable estimate of symptom severity.

Second, although the internal consistency of a particular measure is often a desirable goal, it must be recalled that ADHD is a disorder with three putative symptom domains (inattention, impulsivity, overactivity) and a host of associated problem areas. Thus reliance on instruments that are internally consistent with respect to only one such domain may underrepresent the multiple areas requiring appraisal and intervention. Multidimensional assessment is necessary.

Third, for many years a common critique of research on child psychopathology was the low interdiagnostician reliability for the major categories of behavioral and emotional disturbance (Quay, 1979). More recently, however, the advent of structured interview techniques and the improved, research-based diagnostic criteria exemplified in the latest editions of the *Diagnostic and Statistical Manual of Mental Disorders* (*DSM-III, DSM-III-R,* and *DSM-IV*) have led to improved agreement figures for the diagnosis of such major syndromes as conduct disorder and ADHD. Although kappa (chance-corrected) agreement figures are still far from perfect, the potential for reliable diagnosis has done much to enhance the scientific status of work on ADHD. Yet, as I now discuss, the accuracy or reliability of diagnosis does not guarantee its validity.

Validity

Validity is a far broader construct, referring globally to an instrument's success in measuring what it was intended to measure. Whereas reliability pertains to the "internal" relationships of the assessment tool with itself (over time, across item content, or as utilized by different individuals), validity typically necessitates comparison with some external standard. Because external standards may themselves vary, validity is always context dependent. For example, the same academic readiness instrument may be valid in the sense that it predicts one important criterion variable (e.g., subsequent academic achievement) but may be totally invalid for other purposes (e.g., it does not accurately capture creativity). In other words, stating that an assessment device is "valid" or "invalid" without referring to a specific criterion is too global a statement.

In classical psychometric theory, an instrument's reliability is a necessary, but not a sufficient, condition for its validity. That is, a valid instrument must (at least) be reliable; if it contains large amounts of unsystematic error, it cannot hope to reflect a scientific construct with much meaning. Yet reliability does not guarantee validity. Indeed, an extremely accurate (reliable) weight scale may be quite valid for appraising body mass but completely invalid for the purpose of appraising a child's hair color, happiness, or school achievement.

The simplest, and potentially most misleading, type of validity for psychological or behavioral measures is face validity, reflecting the extent to which an assessment tool appears to relate to the criterion of interest. Whether items "look right" with respect to the criterion is a crude index of validity at best. More important is content validity, or the instrument's representation of the pertinent domain of functioning. A content-valid rating scale to assist with the evaluation of ADHD must include items reflecting various types of attentional performance, both cognitive and behavioral impulsivity, and motoric overactivity. Most references to validity imply criterion-related validity, the instrument's ability to predict independent measures of the same entity. Does a score on a hyperactivity rating scale correlate substantially with a well-established interview measure? Can a child's performance on a computer task purporting to evaluate sustained attention predict teacher ratings or behavior observations of attention in the classroom? Finally, the complex concept of construct validity refers to the tool's ability to accurately measure a pertinent scientific concept, typically requiring both convergent validity (positive criterion-related validity with other measures of the same construct) and divergent or discriminant validity (the measure's failure to correlate with competing constructs).

In the field of ADHD, Jan Loney and colleagues systematically derived measures of inattention-overactivity (IO) and of aggression (A) that are construct valid. That is, they selected rating scale or interview items pertinent to the IO domain only if such items predicted independent measures of this construct and simultaneously failed to predict independently appraised aggression; the converse criteria were applied to items measuring the domain of A (see Loney, 1987; Loney & Milich, 1982, for details). This kind of attention to construct-valid measurement has propelled progress in the field by providing for appropriate separation of the partially independent domains of hyperactivity and aggression (Hinshaw, 1987b).

In sum, developers and users of evaluation tools for ADHD strive for the ideal of assessment instruments that are both reliable and valid. A critical issue for the field, however, is that various informants often disagree in their appraisals of a child's levels of attention deficits and hyperactivity. This topic of cross-informant consistency is of sufficient importance to bear discussion in its own right.

CROSS-INFORMANT CONSISTENCY
IN THE ASSESSMENT OF ADHD

As noted at the outset of this chapter, evaluating multiple domains of functioning and obtaining the perspectives of multiple informants are essential to capture the diversity of ADHD symptomatology. Researchers may rightly ask, however, whether the impressions of different informants converge. Indeed, the issue of cross-informant consistency straddles the border of reliability and validity. The extent to which individuals agree with respect to the child's problem behaviors can be seen as relating both to interinformant agreement (reliability) and to the predictability of functioning in one domain from that in another (criterion-related validity). Such cross-informant consistency of our assessment tools is important at a practical as well as conceptual level: If informants disagree, whose data do we "count" in formulating a diagnosis?

The influential meta-analytic review of Achenbach, McConaughy, and Howell (1987) provides critical information relevant to this topic. These investigators amalgamated information from a large number of studies in which parents, teachers, peers, mental health workers, or children themselves provided assessment information regarding child psychopathology. In brief, when two similar informants—for example, two parents, or a teacher and a teacher's aide—rated the same child, they showed moderate levels of correspondence regarding the child's behavioral or emotional problems, with an average intercorrelation of $r = .6$. Yet when two different adult informants appraised the same youngster, the average association plunged dramatically; the average r between parents and teachers, for example, was below .30. Even lower was the correspondence between a child's self-report and that of adult informants (average $r = .22$). Although all of these correlations are statistically significant given the large number of studies reviewed, the latter correlations are quite modest, signifying a marked lack of correspondence across different informants.[3]

Rather than attributing such small associations to the unreliability of different informants or assessment tools, Achenbach et al. (1987) contended that parents and teachers (for example) view and appraise children in substantially different contexts. Each source, in fact, may be reasonably reliable (in terms of, for example, test-retest reliability) and may provide valid information; the lack of correlation with other informants may relate to the substantial variability of children's actual behavior in divergent situations. Viewed from this perspective, low levels of cross-informant consistency do not simply represent unsystematic error in assessment information but may reinforce the need to obtain data from different informants and different settings to capture the situational variability in the child's behavioral repertoire. In short, each informant may contribute a unique perspective to the evaluation of the child.

In all, the perspective of Achenbach et al. (1987) mandates obtaining evaluation data from all important domains of functioning and from each important informant in the child's life. Following consideration of theoretical frameworks and a focused review of major assessment instruments, I return at the conclusion of the chapter to the critical issue of the amalgamation and integration of information from diverse sources with respect to forming a coherent diagnostic picture.

THEORETICAL FRAMEWORK FOR ASSESSMENT

Assessment of children with attention deficits and hyperactivity cannot take place in the absence of some overarching conceptions about the nature of the disorder—and, indeed, of child psychopathology in general—or without consideration of key psychometric, developmental, and theoretical issues (Mash & Terdal, 1988). Before proceeding to cover major assessment instruments, I briefly address several developmental and theoretical issues that have direct bearing on assessment conceptualization and procedures.

First, as discussed further in Chapter 3, there are a host of intertwined genetic, biological, familial, and sociocultural factors that interact to yield a symptom pattern characteristic of ADHD. In some children, known biological factors may play a relatively strong role; in others, environmental/familial variables may take precedence. Although ascertaining a specific primary cause for a given child's ADHD is not a viable goal of assessment—chiefly because such single, primary causes are likely to exist only in rare cases—and although intervention strategies need not be directed at the primary etiologic factors or agents,[4] our evaluation procedures must reflect adequate coverage of the range of potential predisposing, precipitating, or maintaining factors in order to pinpoint intervention strategies. For instance, high levels of lead in the child with clinically significant attention deficits and hyperactivity require intervention, even if the ADHD symptomatology has other roots as well. Alternatively, marital discord may not have caused core symptoms, but it may well be a maintaining or even exacerbating factor, requiring intervention prior to more traditional behavior management strategies to decrease misbehavior in the child.

It is important to realize, in addition, that such causal factors are likely to interact actively in complex ways. Genetic or nongenetic biological predispositions may correlate with the environments in which the individual functions; environmental influences may directly affect underlying biology (as in lead ingestion, or even in the accumulation of stress, both of which may alter brain functioning). Also, family or school settings may amplify or dampen underlying symptom tendencies. Although an integrated biopsychosocial perspective has been advocated for some time as a goal for psychiatry and clinical psychology (Engel, 1977), as a field we still tend to pursue rather narrowly construed perspectives that are biological *or* familial *or* environmental/social. Yet our assessments must be able to incorporate different areas of functioning as well as disparate causal factors, with the goal of a more complete understanding of distal and proximal influences.

Second, consideration of the dynamic, developmental nature of ADHD symptomatology is crucial for both the individual assessor and the nosologist. Although there is increasing evidence for the persistence of ADHD behavior across development—from preschool years through adolescence and even young adulthood in many cases (Campbell, 1990; Klein & Mannuzza, 1991)—the constituent behaviors of children with ADHD change form with both maturation and shifts in setting parameters. The fussy, irritable, demanding toddler may develop into the inattentive, defiant preschooler with negative parent-child interactions; emerging later is the impulsive, overly active, dysregulated child in grade school who suffers classroom failure and peer rejection. Rather than simply serving as correlates of the disorder, school failure and rejection by agemates may themselves serve to intensify underlying symptom patterns (Hinshaw, 1992b; Parker & Asher, 1987) and trigger greater disorganization of behavior and the emergence of frank antisocial behavior. By adolescence, this hypothetical pattern may shift again, with motoric hyperactivity abating but escalations in social isolation and negative self-esteem emerging in reaction to years of frustration and negative feedback. In short, there is continuity that can be traced in the behavior patterns, but such continuity is displayed via differing manifestations across development. This so called "heterotypic continuity" means that (a) assessment strategies must be geared towards the child's developmental stage, (b) apparent discontinuities in surface behaviors may actually be linked in complex, dynamic fashion, and (c) our nosologies must be able to reflect the shifting nature of symptom patterns over time (see Moffitt, in press, regarding heterotypic continuity in the development of antisocial behavior).

Developmental considerations in the assessment of the child with ADHD are presented quite well by Campbell (1990) and Shelton and Barkley (1990); I mention several points briefly. First, because preschoolers display increased rates of the constituent behaviors of inattention, impulsivity, and overactivity (which gradually decrease with development), the threshold for a diagnosis of ADHD should be raised in this age group. Otherwise, we run the risk of overidentifying such youngsters; a preponderance of false positive diagnoses for 3- to 5-year-olds is clearly not a desirable state of affairs. Yet severe levels of the constituent behaviors in this age range are highly predictive of continuity over time (Campbell, 1990; Richman, Stevenson, & Graham, 1982); it would be an equal mistake to fail to identify developmentally severe manifestations of ADHD in preschoolers. Second, given that ADHD symptomatology is increasingly expressed in educational settings across middle childhood, we must evaluate not only the child's behaviors but also the types of demands and expectations that teachers (and parents) place on the child. Modification of such expectancies may be an important intervention (see Barkley, 1987). Third, as children develop, we must take into account the increasing influence of the peer culture and the particular difficulties that adolescence may bring to the youngster whose core problems lie in the area of self-regulation. Separating disorganization and rebellion that may be normative for many adolescents from manifestations of ADHD will require knowledge of family dynamics as well as a developmentally sensitive assessor. In short, unfolding developmental stages bring new challenges for the ADHD youngster and the assessor alike. With this all-too-brief consideration of theoretical and developmental issues in mind, I now turn to an overview of assessment tools and instruments that may be particularly useful in the evaluation and diagnosis of children with ADHD.

KEY ASSESSMENT TOOLS

The measures discussed here are representative tools pertinent to the evaluation of children with attention deficits and hyperactivity. Although some are exemplary, the inclusion of any instrument does not imply uncritical advocacy, nor does the exclusion of other measures signify their rejection. In short, space does not permit encyclopedic coverage; this list is illustrative rather than exhaustive.

Rating Scales

Rating instruments or questionnaires are perhaps the most widely utilized assessment tools for the evaluation of youngsters with attention problems and hyperactivity. Advantages pertain to their brevity, ease of use, and ability to sample adult informants' impressions of the child's behavior in home or school settings. Rating scales, however, provide only a cross-sectional view of symptomatology; their use for establishing duration of symptom patterns—essential for diagnosis—is limited (Hinshaw & Nigg, in press; Hodges, 1993). Another potential disadvantage is their global nature, which may lead to bias. Specifically, the presence of oppositional or aggressive features in a child may create a "negative halo" in the rater to infer inattentive or hyperactive behaviors even when the latter have not been displayed (Abikoff, Courtney, Pelham, & Koplewicz, in press; Schachar, Sandberg, & Rutter, 1986). In addition, one must pay close attention to the norms on which rating scale cutoff scores are based; an unrepresentative normative sample may either understate or overinflate levels of attention problems and hyperactivity. Furthermore, assessors must examine whether the briefer rating instruments have sufficient item pools and the proper item selection procedures to yield construct-valid indexes of key subdimensions such as inattention, hyperactivity, and aggression. The most commonly used brief rating instrument for ADHD, the 10-item Conners Abbreviated Symptom Questionnaire, which provides a single "hyperkinesis" score, confounds hyperactivity and oppositionality (Ullmann, Sleator, & Sprague, 1985). Despite such concerns and limitations, however, rating scales are an indispensable element of the assessment of children with suspected attention deficits and hyperactivity. Comprehensive coverage of the various rating instruments is found in such sources as Barkley (1990), Hinshaw and Nigg (in press), and a special issue of the *Psychopharmacology Bulletin* (1985) that reviewed rating scales for use in child psychopharmacology research.

Broad scales related to wide conceptions of child psychopathology are valuable for their coverage of not only inattention and hyperactivity but also aggression, antisocial behavior, and internalizing features, to provide a comprehensive picture of behavioral and emotional functioning. The extensively normed and investigated Child Behavior Checklist (Achenbach, 1991) is the paradigmatic rating scale for the field. Its current revision features a consistent factor structure for parent and teacher versions of the instrument as well as for males and females of different age ranges, affording comparability of scores across development and across key informants. Narrow-band scales relevant to the externalizing domain include attention problems, aggression, and delinquency; several internalizing scales are also included, as is a section related to socially competent functioning. Other broad scales in wide use are the Revised Behavior Problem Checklist of Quay and Peterson (1983), which can be completed by parents as well as teachers, and the Conners Parent Rating Scale and the Conners Teacher Rating Scale (Goyette, Conners, & Ulrich, 1978).

Narrower scales related solely to externalizing behavior include the Conners Abbreviated Symptom Questionnaire, a 10-item scale also known as the "Hyperkinesis Index" that contains frequently endorsed and medication-sensitive items from the longer Conners instruments. As noted above, its total score tends to select youngsters with considerable oppositionality or aggression in addition to hyperactivity. In an attempt to construct a brief scale with construct-valid dimensions of inattention-overactivity versus aggression, Loney and Milich (1982) began with items from the lengthier Conners Parent and Teacher Rating Scales. By selecting only those items that specifically related to one or the other domain, they constructed two 5-item indexes comprising the IOWA Conners Scale. Also, the items from the *DSM-III-R* criteria for ADHD (as well as for oppositional-defiant disorder and conduct disorder) have been transformed into a rating scale format by Pelham, Gnagy, Greenslade, and Milich (1992); preliminary norms are provided. Space does not permit discussion of the many additional narrow scales that have been created.

In sum, rating scales constitute an ideal "first wave" of assessment data pertinent to attention deficits, hyperactivity, and additional symptomatology. Importantly, they sample the impressions of key adults regarding the child's typical behavior patterns in the natural environment, without requiring extensive training. They tap key symptoms and may help to ascertain important syndromal manifestations; but without supplemental assessment that allows systematic information on symptom onset and additional diagnostic categories, they are of limited use for careful diagnosis. The ease of administration of the briefer scales is well suited for repeated assessments during treatment programs, but their coverage of additional psychopathology is limited. If their limitations are respected, and particularly if the assessor is knowledgeable about the normative basis of the cutoff scores that a given scale utilizes, rating scales can be quite useful in initiating an assessment package and in aiding the monitoring of treatment response.

Interviews

Two general types of interviews are utilized with regard to the assessment and diagnosis of child psychopathology. First, unstructured clinical interviews allow the informants (usually the parents or teachers) to provide their own views of the child's impact upon the home or school and to give voice to their frustrations and concerns with the bothersome patterns of misbehavior that typically prompt referral. Despite their flexibility and their focus on the respondent's concerns—making them ideal for initial clinic consultations—such unstructured interviews are quite unreliable with respect to obtaining a diagnosis. This contention is understandable if one considers the wide fluctuations in such factors as respondent mood and perspective and in interviewer orientation and style that may accrue to open-ended interviews.

Over the past decade and a half, structured diagnostic interviews, in which questions are asked in a prearranged formula emphasizing rigor and consistency, have gained increasing support as more reliable means of assessing child psychopathology when diagnosis is an important goal. Such structured interviews are particularly helpful for ascertaining a definitive diagnosis of ADHD as well as the full range of possible comorbid diagnoses that may accompany ADHD. Indeed, the sole use of rating scales is insufficient when the goal is to determine formal diagnostic status because such questionnaires are inadequate for ascertaining the duration of problematic behaviors. Differential diagnosis is also aided by structured interviews, in that symptoms that may be common to multiple disorders (e.g., concentration problems that may accompany depression) can be linked with other presenting behaviors to yield coherent syndromes or disorders.[5]

Structured interviews are most often administered to parents, although for the externalizing disorders teacher administration is desirable, given the salience of the classroom for the display of inattention, impulsivity, and hyperactivity. A major question pertains to the reliability and validity of the child's self-report. Whereas the reliability of structured interviews with children under 9 years is typically below acceptable standards, for youngsters above this age interviews may be essential for obtaining valid information about both internalizing features and anti-social behavior. Adults will often be ignorant of the child's internal state or his or her commission of antisocial acts; teachers, in particular, are not optimal informants regarding internalizing features (Hinshaw, Han, Erhardt, & Huber, 1992). As noted at the outset of this chapter, however, children of any age are extremely likely to underreport problems in the domain of attention deficits, impulsivity, and hyperactivity (Loeber, Green, Lahey, & Stouthamer-Loeber, 1991). Whether to perform a formal interview with the child depends on his or her age as well as the domains of functioning that require elucidation. In short, although self-report for ascertaining symptoms of ADHD is apt to be of extremely limited value, the child's perspective on other domains of functioning may be crucial.

The most widely used structured interviews for child psychopathol-ogy are listed in Table 2.1. The most researched instrument is the Diagnostic Interview Schedule for Children (DISC), an extremely struc-tured interview that was devised for lay interviewers in epidemiologic investigations. Its latest revision, the DISC-2, is keyed to *DSM-III-R* (Fisher et al., 1991); the DISC-3 (keyed to *DSM-IV*) is slated for release in 1994. Parent versions of all of these instruments share roughly com-parable reliability data with respect to externalizing diagnoses such as ADHD, with obtained interdiagnostician agreement figures for anxiety and depressive disorders that are substantially lower. The validity of diagnostic interviews is typically assessed in relation to alternative diag-nostic formulations that share similar sources of underlying data; thus, as in other domains of clinical psychology and psychiatry, validation efforts suffer from the lack of a true "gold standard." An authoritative review of current diagnostic interviews for child psychopathology is found in Hodges (1993).

Finally, additional interviews focus on domains other than psycho-pathology per se. For example, semistructured interviews regarding parental impressions of the child's developmental history are of critical importance for ascertaining key information about motoric, cognitive, self-care, and language performance earlier in the child's history (see Barkley, 1990). Indeed, if there were to be only one assessment tool that could be used to evaluate the child who potentially has ADHD, a thorough developmental and family history might well be the choice, given its potential richness, its coverage of associated symptom fea-tures, its provision of information regarding crucial contextual factors,

TABLE 2.1 Structured Diagnostic Interviews for Assessing Child
　　　　　　　　Psychopathology

Instrument	Reference
Diagnostic Interview Schedule for Children (DISC-2)	Fisher et al. (1991)
Schedule for Affective Disorders and Schizophrenia for School-aged Children (K-SADS)	Puig-Antich & Chambers (1978)
Diagnostic Interview for Children and Adolescents (DICA)	Herjanic, Herjanic, Brown, & Wheatt (1975)
Child and Adolescent Psychiatric Assessment (CAPA)	Angold, Cox, Prendergast, Rutter, & Simonoff (1987)
Child Assessment Schedule (CAS)	Hodges, Kline, Stern, Cytryn, & McKnew (1982)

NOTE: See Hodges (1993) for a thorough review of such instruments.

and its ability to rule in or rule out a host of potential risk factors and causal agents.

Behavior Observations

Although quite costly and difficult to coordinate logistically, systematic behavior observations in the natural environment yield the potential advantage of more precise and objective evaluation of key behavioral tendencies than is obtainable from rating scales. Observer teams perform repeated observations of children in class or play settings, or in the home, recording at regular intervals the salient behaviors of interest. The relatively low levels of inference required to check the appropriate behavioral category often yield frequency counts of important classes of behavior that are fairly distinct from other classes.[6] Importantly for intervention, behavior observations can address not only inattentive, off-task, and overactive behaviors but also such important domains as interpersonal aggression, social isolation, and social skills (Hinshaw, Henker, Whalen, Erhardt, & Dunnington, 1989). For systematic intervention studies with ADHD children, behavior observations have served as key outcome measures (e.g., Gittelman et al., 1980; Hinshaw, Henker, & Whalen, 1984a).

The Classroom Behavior Observation Code of Abikoff, Gittelman-Klein, and Klein (1977) and the class, lunchroom, and playground observational system of Gadow and colleagues (Gadow, Nolan, Sverd, Sprafkin, & Paolicelli, 1990) are representative of validated behavior observation systems in the field. Because systematic behavior observation efforts require substantial training of key personnel and multiple observers to obtain checks on interobserver reliability, they are outside the window of feasibility for most clinicians. Yet the hope is that school districts, mental health centers, and health maintenance organizations will begin to incorporate traveling observer teams that can be utilized across multiple sites in an attempt to add this crucial methodology to assessment efforts.

Behavior observations of clinic-based interactions or even of solitary clinic behavior are also possible (see Barkley, 1990, for a review). Here, parent-child interchanges (Barkley & Cunningham, 1979), peer group interactions (Pelham & Bender, 1982), and solitary playroom behavior (Roberts, 1990) can be either observed from behind a one-way mirror or coded from videotapes. Although coding can be arduous, the potential yield with respect to reliable, objective information on discrete behaviors or key interactional processes may be quite large. Again, despite the potential issue of the generalizability of clinic-based observations to the natural environment, the hope is that observing direct interactions of such key areas as parent-child interchange or peer group behavior will yield more specific and valid information than will adult impressions from rating scales.

Tests of Cognitive, Intellectual, and Achievement-Related Functioning

Given the above-noted difficulties with school performance that pertain to an extremely large percentage of children with ADHD, evaluation of intellectual potential and of current academic achievement is often indicated for this population. Such evaluation must be individually administered by a trained examiner. Assessment tools like the third edition of the Wechsler Intelligence Scale for Children (WISC-III; Wechsler, 1991), the Kaufman Assessment Battery for Children (KABC; Kaufman & Kaufman, 1983), the Woodcock-Johnson Psychoeducational Battery-Revised (Woodcock & Johnson, 1989-1990), and the recent Wechsler Individual Achievement Test (WIAT; Wechsler, 1992) are well-normed and thorough instruments for the appraisal of intellectual functioning and academic achievement.

Recall, however, that one-on-one administration of such instruments may not capture the full range of inattentive and overactive symptomatology that is typically exhibited in the natural environment. For teacher appraisal of the child's actual academic work in the classroom, the Academic Performance Rating Scale of DuPaul, Rapport, and Perriello (1991) yields reliable and valid information that is quite specific. In addition, actual products of the child (school work samples, grades, curriculum-based assessment via microcomputers) may serve as key evaluation data.

Beyond the basic evaluation of intellectual functioning and school performance, a wide range of neuropsychological instruments has been utilized with ADHD youngsters, but (a) such evaluation is often quite costly and (b) the specification of interventions based on a particular neuropsychological profile is not firmly established (Gittelman & Feingold, 1983). From a research perspective, hypothesized deficit areas of neuropsychological functioning (particularly those in the frontal lobe area) are not always replicated in samples of ADHD youngsters (Barkley, Grodzinsky, & DuPaul, 1992). The next decade should witness further developments in this field, as increasingly sophisticated neuropsychological tools are utilized to localize deficit areas in children with ADHD and underachievement (Barkley, in press).

Peer Sociometric Evaluations

Although not typically obtained as part of a clinical assessment, sociometric assessments from peers may be particularly important prognostically. As noted earlier, ADHD children are particularly likely to receive rejection from agemates, which is a potent predictor of negative course. Because teacher estimates of a child's peer status are only partially valid, obtaining information on social preferences directly from children is far preferable, even though such data collection may be outside the scope of most practitioners. Reviews of current sociometric procedures for use with children are found in Asher and Coie (1990) and Newcomb, Bukowski, and Pattee (1993).

Laboratory Measures of Attention,
Impulsivity, and Hyperactivity

As explored in Hinshaw (1987a), Barkley (1991), and Pelham and Milich (1991), laboratory measures of the key constructs of attentional deployment, impulse control deficits, and motoric overactivity are still largely in the research/experimental stage, with little clinical utility established. Whereas such tools as computerized measures of cognitive functions believed to underlie attentional deficits, biological assays of key neurotransmitters and metabolites, and a host of indexes of hyperactivity promise to yield important insights into underlying mechanisms of the disorder, few are sufficiently validated to be useful for clinical decision making pertinent to the individual case. Use of computerized tests of attention deployment, for example, will yield both false positive predictions (child without ADHD who shows inattention) and false negative predictions (child with ADHD who shows adequate attention). The reader is advised to research any such laboratory measures carefully before deciding to include them in assessment batteries for clinical evaluation. In discussing the nature of ADHD, I consider several of these types of measures further in Chapter 3.

Competencies

All children, even those with clinically significant attention deficits and hyperactivity, have areas of strength as well as weakness. Given the litany of problems that are associated with ADHD, it may become easy to overlook the competencies such children display, but evaluation of this domain is also crucial. The field of developmental psychopathology is coming to the realization that the study of behavioral disturbance may be optimally informed by focus on children's resiliency in the face of stress (Garmezy, 1989). Identification of protective factors—those variables that, even under conditions of risk, predict healthy outcomes—is therefore critical. Also, for the purpose of implementing psychosocial intervention programs, assessors must identify a child's areas of strength because these may constitute alternative skills, incompatible with problem behavior, that should serve as intervention targets. Knowing about the child's strengths may also help to ascertain reinforcers for behavioral programs. Finally, a focus on strengths may be essential in bolstering a child's flagging self-esteem. In brief, the area of children's positive features and competencies should not be overlooked.

AMALGAMATING DISPARATE
SOURCES OF INFORMATION

Given the diversity of assessment information required for a thorough evaluation of the youngster with ADHD, and particularly given the need for different informants to contribute to the database, an essential issue is how best to amalgamate and synthesize the potentially divergent information that is obtained. If, for example, parents describe markedly defiant and impulsive behavior at home, but the teacher discusses an attentive, thoughtful child, what is the potential resolution? Alternatively, how does the assessor contend with disparities between the child's self-report (essentially denying problem behavior), testing data (indicating mild attentional problems), and the teacher's contention that the child cannot focus on academic material in class for more than 5 minutes? As noted in an earlier section of this chapter, interinformant agreement is quite modest with regard to child psychopathology, yet Achenbach et al. (1987) contend that this lack of overlap does not necessarily signal unreliability but rather the expression of unique perspectives from informants who witness divergent behavior. How is the assessor to integrate disparate information?

No easy solution is apparent for such dilemmas. Certainly, if sound data exist to the effect that, for example, children's self-reports markedly underestimate ADHD symptomatology (Loeber, Green, Lahey, & Stouthamer-Loeber, 1991), such evidence may be a guide suggesting the discounting of this source and the inclusion of parent and teacher reports if the behaviors in question are noted. Yet it is quite difficult to establish the ultimate criterion measure against which to appraise the soundness of any particular source. In other words, a "gold standard" that is independent of the typical sources used to establish a diagnosis rarely exists. Achenbach (1990) has suggested that, for nosologies of child disorders, the five axes should refer not to major mental disorders, developmental disorders, medical conditions, psychosocial stressors, and global adaptation (see American Psychiatric Association, 1987) but to a particular source of assessment information. In his proposal, the axes would represent parent information, teacher data, results of cognitive and psychological assessments, physical examination, and the child's self-report. This proposal for a multiaxial nosologic framework based on the source of assessment data explicitly recognizes the diversity of perspectives of different informants.

A major goal for the field is to ascertain appropriate means of combining data from the various sources when they do not converge. Although formulas for ascertaining the proper blends of different informants' data can be generated, complex multivariate combinations may not necessarily be optimal. A helpful perspective on this topic is presented by Piacentini, Cohen, and Cohen (1992), who emphasize, on methodologic grounds, that simple algorithms are nearly always preferable to complicated weightings of various sources. An example of such a "simple" algorithm is to "count" a symptom when any one source has indicated its presence. As the field increasingly recognizes that no one source of assessment information has automatic primacy, this area should receive increasing attention from investigators and clinicians.

SUMMARY

Assessment related to children with attention deficits and hyperactivity requires the use of reliable and valid instruments that sample behavior in the natural settings in which key problem areas are displayed. The usual clinic-based procedures—which entail one-on-one evaluation of cognition, achievement, medical problems, and emotional functioning —typically do not reveal the types of difficulties ADHD children display in home, school, and peer settings, mandating use of interview and rating scale procedures with parents, teachers, and even agemates. A thorough developmental history and a comprehensive review of functioning in key domains are essential aspects of diagnostic and assessment procedures. I briefly reviewed the potential utility of rating instruments, interviews, behavior observations, peer reports, individual assessments of cognition and neuropsychological performance, and laboratory measures for sampling the child's skills and deficits in critical areas of functioning. To aid with intervention, competencies and strengths of the child and in the environment must also be ascertained. Overall, in formulating a diagnosis, there is no substitute for thorough knowledge of (a) child psychopathology in general, to help in making differential diagnostic decisions; (b) the psychometric properties of the various assessment tools that can be utilized to sample behavior in the child's natural environment; and (c) the variety of assessments of ancillary areas of functioning, including speech and language skills, cognitive development, and neuropsychological functioning, to name several. Currently, given relatively low levels of agreement about the child's behavior from different sources—which may signal the variability of child behavior as much as the reliability of the instruments—the field is formulating means of amalgamating information from the diverse informants and procedures that provide key information.

NOTES

1. Recent, unpublished data from my laboratory give additional testimony to the poor self-monitoring abilities of ADHD youngsters. Utilizing an original self-report measure of children's aggressive tendencies (Zupan, 1991), Hinshaw and Garcia (unpublished data) found that self-reported aggression differentially correlated with objective observations of verbal and physical aggression (during naturalistic summer camp programs) for ADHD and comparison samples. Specifically, the association between self-reported aggression and observed aggression in the comparison boys was $r = .44$, but the correlation

for ADHD boys was $r = .04$. These significantly different correlations signify the low accuracy of self-report of the ADHD youngsters—who were observed to be six times as aggressive as the comparison boys.

2. When multiple diagnosticians or observers are compared regarding their decisions as to the presence or absence of a particular diagnosis, calculation of reliability must take into account the agreement that could have occurred by chance alone. For example, if the children in a given sample have either ADHD or no diagnosis, and if the base rate (i.e., frequency of occurrence) of ADHD is 40%, the diagnosticians would agree solely by chance 16% of the time (the probability of the joint occurrence of two independent events equals the product of their separate occurrences; $40\% \times 40\% = 16\%$). Kappa is a statistic that reflects the obtained interobserver or interdiagnostician agreement that transcends the rate of chance agreements; it equals the obtained agreement minus the chance agreement divided by one minus the chance agreement.

3. Achenbach et al. (1987) found that the average cross-informant correlations were somewhat stronger for the appraisal of externalizing (hyperactive, aggressive) than for internalizing (social withdrawal, anxiety, depression) behavior patterns. More overt, "visible" psychopathology is thus apparently somewhat easier for observers to notice. Still, however, cross-informant correspondence for this domain is modest.

4. Phenylketonuria (PKU) is a genetic defect that causes the individual to be unable to metabolize phenylalanine, buildup of which in the system can lead to mentally retarded functioning. Yet the primary intervention, given current inability to perform genetic therapies, is solely "environmental": Phenylalanine is withheld from the diet. By this measure retardation may be minimized or prevented. In short, effective interventions that are not directed at primary causal factors may be quite efficacious.

5. Because of the omnipresence of attentional problems and overactivity in child psychopathology, performing differential diagnoses is indeed of crucial importance. For detailed information regarding the separation (and linkages) between ADHD and such frequently associated conditions as learning disabilities, ODD, CD, and internalizing disorders, see Barkley (1990).

6. In my summer research programs for boys with ADHD, I have utilized both rating scales and direct observations of overt aggression, covert antisocial behavior, and prosocial interaction. Whereas the observational codes of these domains are intercorrelated with mild to moderate magnitude—attesting to their partial independence—parallel dimensions from the rating scales are so highly associated (r's $= .85$ and above) as to be collinear, precluding analyses of the separate domains.

3

THE NATURE OF
THE DISORDER AND
ETIOLOGIC HYPOTHESES

The goals for this chapter are to explore the nature of ADHD and to examine current conceptions regarding the etiology of the condition. Although clear answers for each topic have eluded investigators for as long as attention deficits and hyperactivity have been studied, in recent years research regarding the essential nature of ADHD has intensified, revealing insights into possible underlying mechanisms. Furthermore, an increasing array of potential causal factors has been identified.

Regarding the nature of ADHD, key questions include the following: What are attentional deficits, and do they actually comprise the core problem area for this diagnostic category? How does one conceptualize impulsivity and disinhibition? Are youngsters with an ADHD diagnosis really "hyperactive"? Which, if any, of these core symptoms occurs more frequently in children with ADHD than in agemates with other behavioral or emotional disorders? Which underlying processes might account for the core symptom patterns as well as for ADHD children's great variability in task performance, their associated problems in achievement and peer relations, and their poor prognosis? Tentative answers to these provocative questions are beginning to emerge.

As for potential etiologic agents and risk factors, I first distinguish types and levels of causation and I next make clear that diverse etiologies exist for the disorder currently named ADHD. Indeed, clearly specified primary causes have been discerned for only small subgroups of ADHD youngsters; etiologic hypotheses increasingly involve transactional models involving complex paths linking biological and environmental factors. In discussing evidence for various causal agents, I also point out the difficulties involved in discerning truly causal factors from correlates or consequences of attention deficits and hyperactivity.

METHODOLOGIC AND
CONCEPTUAL ISSUES

Considerable methodologic and conceptual problems have hindered pertinent investigations of the nature and etiology of ADHD. First, the fluctuating terminology and diverse diagnostic criteria employed over the past decades (see Chapter 1) have made it particularly difficult to know whether a given mechanism (e.g., sustained attention) or etiologic factor (e.g., perinatal difficulties) is being applied to the same types of children across different investigations. Indeed, given nonstandard and changing diagnostic practices, there should be little wonder at the continuing failure, over the years, to replicate key findings in the field (e.g., Zametkin & Rapoport, 1987). Even today, the more rigorous and empirically tested criteria utilized in the *Diagnostic and Statistical Manual of Mental Disorders* are far from fully reliable, specific, or valid. Furthermore, the lack of reporting of additional diagnoses in many investigations renders problematic the comparability of a given ADHD sample with others in the literature (see Chapter 4 for elaboration of issues regarding comorbidity). Unless standard diagnostic procedures are utilized, the field will continue to aim its probes about underlying mechanisms and causal variables at moving targets, that is, at diverse children who may mistakenly receive the same diagnostic label.

Second, whereas various mechanisms or etiologic factors have often been shown to differentiate ADHD from comparison youngsters, it is quite rare for investigators to include psychiatric comparison groups in their studies. Without such groups, any symptom cluster, psychopathological mechanism, or potential etiologic factor that distinguishes hyperactive from nondiagnosed youngsters may not be specific to ADHD. In such cases, we are left with knowledge about the general nature of child behavior disorders, or about the effects of a child's receipt of a label, but information about whether the construct in question actually relates to ADHD is lacking. For example, as I soon discuss, deficits in attention or concentration appear to apply to a number of childhood conditions. The message to the field is that only studies including psychiatric comparison groups are likely to advance knowledge of the specific nature and specific causes of ADHD. However, the few such reports performed to date have often failed to corroborate the specificity of suspected correlates, risk factors, or causal agents (see, for example, Halperin, Matier, Bedi, Sharma, & Newcorn, 1992; Milich & Dodge, 1984; Werry, Elkind, & Reeves, 1987). The search for specific manifestations of this (or any other) diagnostic category in child psychopathology is not yielding simple answers.

Finally, most investigations regarding causal factors rely on cross-sectional or retrospective research methodologies, in which already-diagnosed ADHD and comparison youngsters are compared with respect to contemporaneous (e.g., family interactions) or prior (e.g., birth history; retrospective accounts of early temperament) variables believed to be related to etiology. With cross-sectional methodologies, a key difficulty should be immediately apparent: Any variable that differentiates groups may be a consequence of the disorder rather than a cause. The truism that correlations do not imply causal connections is particularly pertinent for investigations in child psychopathology. For example, the greater family discord and stress in ADHD samples may reflect parental reaction to an impulsive, defiant child rather than a primary cause of the deviant child behavior (Anastopoulos et al., 1992; see also discussion later in this chapter).[1] Without knowledge of parent-child interactions prior to the development of ADHD symptomatology, we cannot know whether earlier family disharmony shaped the initial display of problem behaviors. Prospective investigations of young children who do not yet display diagnosable ADHD are highly desirable, yet such studies incur a host of logistic and budgetary problems. Overall, the barriers to establishing and confirming etiologic factors for attention deficits and hyperactivity are formidable.

THE NATURE OF ADHD: UNDERLYING MECHANISMS

Do the Core Features of ADHD Cluster Together?

In Chapter 1, I briefly discussed recent factor analyses of parent and teacher ratings of the core symptoms of inattention, impulsivity, and hyperactivity, results of which have implications for the existence of underlying patterns of the constituent behaviors. Results converge on the finding that the underlying symptoms fall into two core dimensions rather than three. Specifically, (a) inattention, cognitive impulsivity (e.g., disorganization, need for teacher's supervision), and occasionally restlessness load together on one factor, whereas (b) problems of motoric overactivity and behavioral disinhibition (impulsivity) form another, orthogonal dimension (Bauermeister, Alegria, Bird, Rubio-Stipec, & Canino, 1992; Lahey, Pelham, et al., 1988). These results are corroborated by results of recent cluster analytic work, in which empirically homogeneous groups of children are formed with respect to the constituent behaviors. Hart et al. (1993) discerned one cluster of children with exclusive deficits in attention, in distinction to another, larger group displaying both inattention/disorganization and impulsivity/hyperactivity (see Chapter 4 for more explicit consideration of subtypes). Similar results were obtained by Lahey, Pelham, et al. (1988). Overall, it appears that two stable dimensions consistently appear, requiring modification of our thinking about the nature of both impulsivity and ADHD as a whole.

Another important issue pertains to the coherence or validity of laboratory measures of the core features of ADHD. Such measures are particularly valued because of their apparent objectivity (see discussion in Chapter 2). If, for example, computerized attention tasks, response search tests measuring impulsivity, and observations of hyperactive behavior were all to converge, the field might stand on firmer scientific footing. Empirical reports, however, reveal a substantial lack of correspondence across such measures, a finding that has raised serious concerns regarding the validity of ADHD (see Rutter, 1983, for a review).

Such poor convergence, however, may relate more to the nature of laboratory assessments than to the viability of ADHD itself. Laboratory indices of a particular domain often show extremely modest associations with other measures of that very domain. Computerized measures of attentional performance do not, in fact, show strong association with teacher ratings of ability to concentrate in class; cognitive measures of impulsivity from computer tasks relate only marginally to indices of behavioral impulsivity. Thus the inability of laboratory attention variables to correspond with laboratory measures of impulsivity may tell us less about the lack of coherence of ADHD than about the selectivity and poor ecological validity of the laboratory measures themselves (Barkley, 1991; Rutter, 1983).[2]

With such preliminary issues in mind, I turn now to discussion of the nature of the primary or core symptom areas of ADHD. After systematically reviewing evidence regarding the scientific status and specificity of these features, I proceed to consider other mechanisms or explanations regarding the nature of ADHD symptomatology.

Core Features

Inattention. Cognitive psychology has long told us that attention is not a unitary construct (for a review, see Voeller, 1991). Indeed, several disparate types of attention are salient, including (but not limited to) selective attention, the ability to attend to a particular stimulus in the presence of other competing stimuli; attentional capacity, the amount of information in short-term memory to which the child can attend; and sustained attention, the persistence of focus over lengthy time periods or during the presence of fatigue. Since the seminal work of Douglas in the 1970s (see review of Douglas, 1983), a prevalent belief has been that ADHD children's most salient problems with attention fall in the area of vigilance or sustained attention. Specifically, with the continuing presentation of repetitive stimuli, the ADHD child's performance— initially equivalent to that of comparison youngsters—will begin to deteriorate, signifying deficiencies in the maintenance of attentional focus. Douglas's (1983) careful elaboration of the precise types of tasks that best differentiate hyperactive from comparison youngsters placed the greatest weight on effortful tasks demanding the maintenance of attention over time.[3]

Such laboratory evidence appears to be bolstered by clinical observations of ADHD children. These youngsters appear to tire rapidly under demanding work loads. Furthermore, although their performance may be optimized when they perform self-paced tasks of their own choosing (e.g., building a model, playing a video game), when demands are paced by others, and particularly when the tasks are not intrinsically interesting, performance fades. Thus the sustained attention hypothesis has clinical appeal as well.

A number of investigations, however, have failed to uncover this supposed deficit in sustained attention in hyperactive or ADHD youngsters (e.g., O'Daugherty, Nuechterlein, & Drew, 1984; Schachar, Logan, Wachsmuth, & Chajczyk, 1988). Among the most prolific critics of this perspective are Sergeant, van der Meere, and colleagues in the Netherlands. In a programmatic series of articles (see particularly Sergeant & Scholten, 1985; van der Meere, van Baal, & Sergeant, 1989; van der Meere, Wekking, & Sergeant, 1991), these investigators have found that, with differing types of tasks related to sustained attention, the performance of ADHD children does not dissipate over time any more than that of comparison youngsters. That is, processing deficits in "resource allocation" that are displayed by ADHD children appear from the earliest moments of task performance, remaining consistently deficient over time; specific problems with sustained attention are not apparent. Indeed, through sophisticated analysis of various components of attention and performance, van der Meere et al. (1989) have inferred that the key factor distinguishing ADHD children from both comparison and learning-disabled youngsters includes deficits in motor output rather than attentional parameters. In short, the ADHD group is most clearly distinguished by slowness in response output, implicating motor-intentional systems as an underlying mechanism (see also Voeller, 1991). The overall interpretation is that ADHD is characterized by difficulties in regulatory control of behavior but not by deficits in sustained attention.

In the United States, Halperin and colleagues have undertaken a systematic program of research to understand attentional difficulties. A bit of detail regarding this work may give a flavor of research on attentional processes. The task they utilize is a modification of a standard continuous performance test, in which the child is instructed to respond, on a computer screen, to a "target" stimulus with one response and to a "nontarget" stimulus by withholding the response. Specifically the child is told to press "X" after every presentation of an "A," but not to respond to any other letter. Incorrect responses are typically grouped into those considered inattentive (failures to respond to the "A" stimulus, or omissions) versus impulsive (responses to stimuli other than "A," or commissions). Through careful examination of response patterns and reaction times, however, Halperin, Wolf, Greenblatt, and Young (1991) discovered that "X-only" responses that are typically considered errors of commission—in which the child hits the response key following a letter different from "A"—actually occur at slow reaction times and correlate with teacher reports of inattention (see also Halperin et al., 1988). Presumably, the child fails to attend to the preceding letter and then subsequently hits "X." It is apparent from this discussion that the linking of particular laboratory responses to underlying response classes of inattention or impulsivity is a difficult process requiring careful consideration of theory and data.

Pertinent to the present discussion, such laboratory inattention was found in both a well-diagnosed group of children with ADHD *and* a psychiatric comparison group composed of youngsters with CD, ODD, anxiety disorders, or affective disorders (Halperin et al., 1992). In other words, the index of inattentive performance was not specific to an ADHD sample, whereas impulsive responses on the continuous performance test were found only in the ADHD youngsters and not in the psychiatric comparison group (see below). Again, this work signifies the importance of precise specification of variables in experimental work in the field. But other careful investigations continue to reveal deficits in the vigilance of ADHD children (e.g., Seidel & Joschko, 1990). Even slight differences in task parameters or in sample composition may be responsible for the inconsistent findings. Clearly, further research with conceptually valid indexes of inattention is needed, and the collaboration of cognitive scientists with investigators interested in ADHD is necessary to yield important benefits with respect to the specification of attention deficits. In all, serious challenges to the primacy of sustained attention deficits in ADHD have been mounted, revealing scientific progress but also indicating the confusing nature of the constructs under consideration.

Impulsivity. In a seminal review paper, Milich and Kramer (1984) discussed the wide variety of measures utilized to measure the construct of impulsivity as well as the lack of correspondence of such measures with one another. The construct of impulsivity is quite likely to be multifaceted. As discussed above, factor analyses of parent and teacher ratings of ADHD-related behavior show that items reflecting the *DSM-III* construct of impulsivity have not cohered: Those measuring a child's need for supervision in class and lack of organization (so-called cognitive impulsivity) load on dimensions marked by inattentiveness, whereas so-called behavioral impulsivity (e.g., calling out in class, failing to consider consequences of actions) cluster with motoric hyperactivity. Furthermore, paper-and-pencil tasks designed to measure cognitive impulsivity are not strongly linked with more ecologically valid indicators of impulsive responding. As thoughtfully argued by Milich and Kramer (1984), impulsivity is a construct in need of further specification.

Three issues pertinent to impulsivity will be discussed briefly. First, reflecting and extending a host of investigations of ADHD youngsters' tendencies towards impulsive cognitive responding on laboratory measures, a carefully selected index of cognitive impulsivity from a laboratory continuous performance task did differentiate ADHD from psychiatric comparison children (Halperin et al., 1992). Second, the above-noted distinction between behavioral and cognitive impulsivity may be quite important. In a well-designed investigation of preadolescent children, White et al. (in press) examined a wide range of cognitive tests and behavioral indicators, discovering that a cognitive versus a behavioral factor of impulsivity emerged. Critically, both cognitive and behavioral impulsivity predicted achievement difficulties in this sample, but only the behavioral dimension predicted antisocial behavior. Behavioral impulsivity may therefore be specifically linked with increased risk for aggressive, antisocial responding.

Third, what has typically been termed behavioral impulsivity may reflect a more global process of disinhibition, which could explain not only quick, careless responding but (a) poor delay of gratification and (b) dysregulated motor activity and other undercontrolled aspects of ADHD (Barkley, in press; Voeller, 1991). Recent work links behavioral disinhibition specifically with ADHD and not with conduct disorder status of adolescents (Milich, Hartung, Martin, & Haigler, 1993). Psychobiological theories are increasingly being invoked to account for such disinhibitory processes (Barkley, in press; Quay, 1988; Voeller, 1991). In short, the role of disinhibition or behavioral impulsivity may integrate existing data and provide a theoretical framework for subsequent research on the nature of ADHD (Barkley, in press).

Motoric Overactivity. Previous reviews of the role of hyperactivity per se concluded that overactive behavior was not omnipresent in youngsters with ADHD but tended to occur only in situations calling for inhibition of motor responses, such as structured classroom settings (Whalen & Henker, 1976). The database for such conclusions, however, typically included studies utilizing behavior observation methods or stabilimetric devices ("wiggle cushions") that measure in-seat movement in class or playroom settings. With the advent of more sophisticated actigraph methods in the 1980s, whereby relatively unobtrusive computerized recorders of body movement could be worn throughout all of a day's activities, it was discovered that youngsters with ADHD displayed greater amounts of motoric activity than comparison children during each period of the day, including sleep (Porrino et al., 1983). Importantly, the largest differences in activity between ADHD and comparison children did occur during structured classroom activities, signifying the importance of environmental parameters and highlighting situational differences in the behavior of ADHD youngsters. In all, such research reflects the current perception that hyperactivity per se is a critical aspect of the disorder.

The renewed belief in the importance of motor activity was emphasized in *DSM-III-R*'s shift in terminology from attention deficit disorder to attention-deficit hyperactivity disorder (American Psychiatric Association, 1987). Two recent investigations bolster this claim. First,

Roberts (1990) carefully analyzed data from playroom observations of ADHD, aggressive, and mixed ADHD-aggressive youngsters who performed solitary free play, restricted play, and academic tasks. Her observational measures, which centered on indices of motor restlessness, out of seat behavior, and grid crossings (overactivity), clearly distinguished the groups; hyperactive and hyperactive-aggressive youngsters displayed far more overactivity and restlessness than did purely aggressive children. In fact, group membership could be accurately predicted from measures of overactivity. Similarly, Halperin et al. (1992) discovered that actigraph-measured overactivity during performance on a computerized attention task characterized ADHD youngsters but not psychiatric or nondiagnosed comparison agemates. Thus, unlike measures of attention span, motor hyperactivity appears to be a specific marker of children with ADHD.

Given the strong empirical linkages between measures of motoric hyperactivity and behavioral impulsivity, recent theoretical perspectives have begun to emphasize the primacy of disinhibitory processes and to suggest that overactivity per se is a manifestation of underlying deficits in delayed responding to various stimuli and in general inhibitory control of behavior (Barkley, in press; see below). Indeed, alternative theoretical constructions of the underlying nature of ADHD have proliferated in recent years.

Alternative Conceptions

Investigators are actively searching for unifying themes that could account for the symptomatology, associated features, and course of ADHD. Although space does not permit full elaboration of any of these models, a brief summary will give perspective on the diversity of theoretical accounts of this condition and on some major unifying themes.

Deficient Self-Regulation. One prevalent view is that ADHD is a disorder marked by poor self-regulatory abilities. That is, the disinhibition and overactivity that appear as primary symptom manifestations, along with the nonspecific but salient attentional deficits that appear in class settings and on laboratory tests, reflect higher order problems with the child's ability to regulate arousal and behavior in accordance with changing environmental demands and to inhibit motoric responses (Douglas, 1983; Voeller, 1991). Although tempting to invoke, this notion could remain at a descriptive level unless the term *self-regulation* is specified. Neuropsychological hypotheses implicating right hemispheric processes involved in response inhibition comprise one such attempt (Voeller, 1991). Another potentially productive avenue involves pertinent theory and research regarding the development of internalized speech in promoting self-control and regulation.

In brief, as the child progresses through the preschool and early elementary years, behavior becomes increasingly regulated as a function of the extent to which adult external control, in the form of verbal commands and prohibitions, becomes "internalized" via overt and then covert self-speech (Berk & Potts, 1991; Luria, 1966). Any delay in such internalized verbal control would be presumably accompanied by a dysregulated, underinhibited behavioral style. Circumstantial evidence for such a perspective comes from the established relationship between ADHD and receptive as well as expressive language delays early in development (Beitchman, Hood, & Inglis, 1990). Perhaps the child with subaverage ability to comprehend or produce language would be lacking in the means to foster internal self-speech that could regulate behavior. Indeed, in a careful examination of the role of self-regulatory private speech in grade-school children with ADHD, Berk and Potts (1991) found evidence for decreased utilization of private speech in ADHD children, particularly in situations that would typically call for effortful information processing.

Yet consensus regarding a clear, unidirectional path from language delay and poor internalization of speech to ADHD has not been established. For one thing, delayed speech and language abilities may alter the nature of parent-child interactions and may engender considerable frustration in the child; thus, causal pathways may include indirect psychosocial factors as well. Also, from an alternate neuropsychological perspective, self-regulation would appear to be a primary function of the frontal lobes, particularly the prefrontal areas. Indeed, evidence exists that explicit frontal lobe damage can lead to a syndrome of dis-. inhibition not unlike many of the core features of ADHD; frontal-lobe etiologic theories are increasingly invoked regarding this disorder. In a systematic literature review, however, Barkley et al. (1992) found marked inconsistency with respect to findings of decreased frontal lobe functioning in youngsters with ADHD. Once again, sampling differences across investigations, potential subgroup differences in response to particular measures, discrepancies in test administration, and conceptual issues regarding the operationalization of frontal lobe functioning may all influence findings. Research density in this area must intensify before the preliminary evidence for frontal lobe involvement in at least some individuals with ADHD (Lou, Henriksen, & Bruhn, 1984; Zametkin et al., 1990) can be confirmed and extended.

Sensitivity to Reward. From a somewhat different perspective, several investigators have examined ADHD children's performance under various conditions of reward. Douglas and Parry (1983), in fact, posited that ADHD is characterized by a heightened sensitivity to reward, making youngsters with the disorder particularly susceptible to performance decrements when partial reinforcement schedules are employed, that is, when frequent reinforcement is thinned to a less dense schedule. This research area is fraught with controversy, however. Another investigative team discovered that ADHD youngsters' performance did not markedly diminish with partial reinforcement, yet the definition of partial reinforcement in this particular report referred to the value of the reinforcers rather than their schedule (Pelham, Milich, & Walker, 1987). Others have speculated that ADHD children are, in fact, undersensitive to both reward and punishment conditions, with consequent difficulties for familial and school socialization (Haenlein & Caul, 1987). In short, despite tantalizing leads, consensus has not emerged in this area of investigation, in part because of the major differences in outcome that even slight definitional or procedural differences regarding "reward" can make in experimental investigations.

Motivational Deficits. In the 1980s Barkley provocatively synthesized many of the above-reported findings pertinent to ADHD into a motivational perspective. That is, invoking Skinnerian notions of stimulus-response linkages, Barkley (1989) claimed that the most parsimonious explanation for the pattern of deficits exhibited by these youngsters is their deficient rule-governed behavior. Under stimulus conditions that would engender compliance from most children, ADHD children fail to complete their performance following presentation of both immediate and prior commands. Rather than requiring explanation at the level of vaguely specified notions of sustained attention, according to Barkley, this pattern more clearly fits a pattern of deficient motivational parameters. This choice of terminology, however, could lead parents and professionals to conclude that youngsters with ADHD are simply uncaring about task completion; and motivation is a notoriously difficult scientific construct to measure, particularly in children. Indeed, a number of investigators, including Barkley, have recently turned their attention to the central role of impulsivity and disinhibitory processes in ADHD.

Disinhibitory Psychopathology. Several trends have precipitated a convergence of opinion and theorizing regarding disinhibition and its importance for ADHD. First, as noted earlier, recent information processing research has implicated poor inhibition of motoric responses rather than attention deficits per se as the defining characteristic of hyperactive children. Second, impulse control problems appear specific to ADHD (e.g., Halperin et al., 1992). Third, by some accounts motoric hyperactivity itself can be viewed as a secondary manifestation of an underlying disinhibitory problem (Barkley, in press). Finally, disinhibited behaviors characterize observations and adult informant ratings of children with ADHD, serving as clear discriminators of ADHD from psychiatric comparison children. In short, what has variously been termed behavioral impulsivity or disinhibition appears to be of crucial importance for ADHD.

What might account for such variegated displays of impulsivity? From a psychobiological perspective, Quay (1988) served the field by explaining and extrapolating from the important and complex neurological theorizing of Gray (1982). Although it is impossible to even begin to capture the essence of this elaborate body of work, of particular relevance to ADHD are Gray's notions of neurally mediated systems of behavioral inhibition and behavioral activation (for a cogent distillation, see McBurnett, 1992). Specific supportive evidence comes from Milich et al. (1993), who found that the performance of adolescents with ADHD on theoretically designed response decision tasks could be explained on the basis of an underactive inhibition system. At a broad level, Barkley (in press) has recently presented an integrative theoretical account of the centrality of disinhibition to ADHD, claiming that the core features and many of the associated problems can be reduced to a primary deficit in delayed responding or impaired response inhibition. Whereas all overarching theories of attention deficits and hyperactivity are likely to run aground on the shoals of high interchild variability and differential subgroup performance (see Chapter 4), neurobiological theory and clinical research are beginning to converge on the importance of disinhibitory psychopathology for ADHD.

Interpersonal Difficulties. From a different perspective, Pelham and Bender (1982), Milich and Landau (1982), and particularly Whalen and Henker (1985, 1992) have made important contributions by focusing our attention on the interpersonal aspects of ADHD. Difficulties with adults and peers, from this perspective, are not peripheral but central aspects of the disorder. Not only are discordant relationships with parents, teachers, and particularly agemates the source of considerable stress— as well as being strongly predictive of later maladjustment (Parker & Asher, 1987)—but difficulties in social interchange may shed light on the nature of the disorder. I note several salient points in this regard.

First, regarding peer relationships, a considerable literature has developed documenting the importance of aggressive behavior in fostering peer rejection (Coie et al., 1990). Indeed, for ADHD children, who develop negative peer reputations after extremely limited periods of contact (Bickett & Milich, 1990; Pelham & Bender, 1982), levels of aggression appear to be the overwhelming factor in mediating such quick disapprobation (Erhardt & Hinshaw, 1993). Yet it is important to note that hyperactive children without significant aggressive behavior are also at strong risk for receiving peer disapproval (Milich & Landau, 1989; Pelham & Bender, 1982). Because peer rejection is ubiquitous for nearly all subgroups of ADHD youngsters, understanding the various reasons for peer rejection across disparate subtypes should be important for understanding underlying mechanisms.

Second, with regard to social skills, ADHD youngsters display few, if any, deficiencies in rates of social interaction, in social cognitive problem solving skills, or in their ability to perceive social situations accurately (Whalen & Henker, 1992). Rather than deficits in social comprehension or social skill, such youngsters appear to display difficulties in the production of appropriate social behavior, as exemplified by their disproportionate rates of socially noxious behavior and their great difficulty in modifying social behavior in accordance with shifting situational demands. Regarding the latter point, ADHD youngsters tend to persist in social roles calling for assertion and dominance even when the situation shifts to call for more deferent or accommodating behavior (Landau & Milich, 1988; Whalen et al., 1979). One explanation is that ADHD children have social agendas that differ from those of their peers; they may, for example, value sensation seeking or social disruption at the expense of smooth interaction as desired goals. Recent data from Melnick and Hinshaw (1993), in fact, confirm that ADHD youngsters (particularly those with comorbid aggression) are likely to voice agendas for social interaction that diverge from those of comparison peers. In all, a social-cognitive perspective on the important social interactional difficulties of ADHD youngsters may begin to yield central clues to the nature of their psychopathology.

Overview

A host of accounts and explanations of ADHD symptomatology have arisen in recent years. Over the past several decades, conceptions of the disorder have evolved on several dimensions, from narrower behavioral symptom clusters to broader notions of deficient self-regulation, and from a focus on lower brain centers (Laufer & Denhoff, 1957) to theories that entail frontal and prefrontal localization (see Hynd, Hern, Voeller, & Marshall, 1991, for elaboration). Another major theme, based on the specificity of impulsivity/overactivity to ADHD samples, involves a central role for disinhibitory psychopathology. Yet attentional difficulties are relevant to this disorder. The recent *DSM-IV* field trials, in which dimensions of inattentive/restless versus impulsive/hyperactive behaviors were separated, revealed that only the inattentive/restless cluster was specifically associated with peer relationship difficulties, whereas impulsive/hyperactive behaviors predicted achievement problems and discordant family relations (Lahey, 1993). In other words, despite their apparent nonspecificity, so-called attention deficits may still be important for ADHD.

Finally, most conceptions of the nature of ADHD have attempted to encompass the entire range of diagnosed children with the disorder, when in fact various subgroups of ADHD youngsters may be quite distinct. ADD without hyperactivity—similar to the inattentive subtype in *DSM-IV*—does not, by definition, entail the types of disinhibitory psychopathology that the majority of ADHD youngsters may display (see Chapter 4 for amplification of subgroup differences). In short, any overarching notions of the underlying mechanisms or nature of ADHD may be so broad as to incur substantial inaccuracy for a meaningful proportion of children. Furthermore, any conceptions of underlying mechanisms must be able to account for a startlingly wide range of problem domains encompassed by youngsters with ADHD, including lower levels of moral reasoning (Simmel & Hinshaw, 1993), frequent academic underachievement (Hinshaw, 1992a), and vast situational fluctuation in the display of symptom patterns (Barkley, in press). Both basic and applied science would be greatly served by appropriate attention to the heterogeneity of the disorder and to its wide array of manifestations.

ETIOLOGY

Preliminary Comments

The caveat noted in the last paragraph can be applied equally to investigations regarding the etiology of ADHD. That is, substantially different causal factors may pertain to diverging subgroups of ADHD children, and qualitatively different sets of risk factors may apply to ADHD children displaying divergent comorbidities with other disorders. In other words, the field must beware of overly global etiologic conceptions for a disorder as diverse as that of ADHD.

Issues regarding the nature of "causation" must be elucidated before specific etiologic hypotheses are addressed. The gold standard for the field involves ascertaining primary causes, those biological or environmental factors that are necessary and sufficient for the display of the disorder. A major genetic finding pertinent to ADHD has recently emerged, in which a genetic condition resulting in generalized resistance to thyroid hormone is strongly associated with reliably diagnosed ADHD but not with other behavior or psychiatric disorders in affected families (Hauser et al., 1993).[4] Yet for most aspects of psychopathology, single-locus genetic determinants are not likely to be confirmed. Any heritable components are quite likely to be polygenic, signifying the influence of multiple, interacting genes on several different chromosomes. Chances for genetic detection and intervention are obviously quite diminished with polygenic transmission. Furthermore, despite the importance of the discovery, the mutant thyroid receptor gene of Hauser et al. (1993) appears to occur with only a tiny prevalence in the population. In short, single, primary causes would appear to operate in only a small proportion of most psychiatric syndromes, including ADHD.

Rather, the field is in the process of identifying (a) predisposing variables—biological or environmental risk factors that occur relatively early in life, incurring vulnerability for the disorder—as well as (b) precipitating events—relatively recent factors that, in combination with predispositions, promote disordered behavior. In so-called diathesis-stress models, both the underlying diatheses (predisposing factors) and stressors (precipitating factors) are needed to create the disorder. In addition to their prominent display in current accounts of such adult disorders as schizophrenia, diathesis-stress would appear to apply to the development of ADHD symptom patterns as well.

Finally, maintaining or escalating factors are neither necessary nor sufficient for the display of disordered behavior, but they may operate to keep in place or exacerbate extant symptom patterns. For example, many investigators believe that discordant family interactions do not comprise primary, predisposing, or precipitating factors for ADHD; rather, these patterns are likely to maintain disorganized, defiant behavior and even to precipitate secondary aggression (e.g., Milich & Loney, 1979). Indeed, such coercive familial interactions may predict the subsequent display of externalizing symptomatology over and above the preexisting symptom levels of the child (Anderson et al., in press; Campbell et al., 1991). Although maintaining factors may seem of secondary importance in the hierarchy of causal events for child psychopathology, it should be remembered that many, if not most, of our treatments are directed at the level of maintaining or escalating factors. In fact, successful intervention with such variables can have clear effects on core symptoms and later course. In all, intervention directed towards primary or predisposing causes is typically precluded either because of the field's ignorance of such causal factors or because of financial and practical constraints on their eradication if they are known; treatment aimed at maintaining factors may have unexpectedly strong benefits.

Another pertinent issue regarding causation is the common belief that causal factors are either biological or environmental in nature. In fact, such "types" of causation are inextricably intertwined. On one side, genetic factors may operate largely through their ability to shape the organism's interchange with the environment, whether the mechanisms are active or passive. Gene-environment correlations are vitally important to specify and study in the field (Caspi & Moffitt, in press; Plomin et al., 1990).[5] From the reverse perspective, so-called environmental influences may have direct effects on underlying biological parameters of the organism. At an obvious level, exposure to environmental toxins may damage brain structures; less apparent, however, are possibilities for positive alterations in brain structure and function as a function of level of environmental stimulation and challenge. The clear message for the field is that attention to complex combinations of intertwined biological and environmental risk factors is essential for elucidating etiology.

A final issue pertains to the nature of investigations that attempt to discern causal factors and the types of inferences made about the validity of various agents. In retrospective studies, the field attempts to ascertain, in identified cases with a certain disorder, the earlier presence of certain etiologic agents or risk factors. High rates of the earlier factor

TABLE 3.1 Contingency Table of Predictors or Causes by Outcomes, Revealing Patterns of Sensitivity, Specificity, and Predictive Power

		Outcome		
		Case	Noncase	
Predictor or	Present	1	2	1 + 2
Putative Causal	Absent	3	4	3 + 4
Factor		1 + 3	2 + 4	

1 = True Positive
2 = False Positive
3 = False Negative
4 = True Negative

1/1 + 3 = Sensitivity (true positives/cases)
1/1 + 2 = Positive Predictive Power (true positives/test positives)
2/2 + 4 = Specificity (true negatives/noncases)
4/3 + 4 = Negative Predictive Power (true negatives/test negatives)

signify the strength of its sensitivity, denoting the proportion of known cases who carry the risk factor. Whereas a sensitive etiologic agent would appear to be quite important, we do not often know, with retrospective designs, how many original individuals with the risk factor went on to develop the condition. In other words, we are not sure of the positive predictive power, signifying the rate of persons with the presumed etiologic agent who later become cases. Only a prospective investigation, which begins before the onset of the disorder, can ascertain this critical statistic (Lewis, 1990). Table 3.1 provides a more detailed representation of the relationships between risk factors/causal agents and clinical outcomes.[6]

To cite a trivial but illustrative example, suppose an investigator examines the presence of ADHD in a given location and finds that 95% of the diagnosed youngsters went to school during the year preceding diagnosis. Here, school attendance has a 95% sensitivity in predicting ADHD! Of course, viewed prospectively, only a small fraction of all children who attend school go on to develop ADHD; the positive predictive power of school attendance will be vanishingly low. In addition, the specificity is also likely to be quite poor, given that nearly all of the noncases of ADHD are also likely to have attended school. The point is that the field may be deceived with respect to the presence of meaningful causal agents unless prospective designs are used and unless careful attention is paid to the positive predictive power and specificity, as well as sensitivity, of putative causes. Unfortunately, given logistic and financial constraints on performing long-term prospective investigations, we know far too little about such statistics for most of the risk factors and suspected causal agents regarding ADHD.

Potential Etiologic Pathways

In this abbreviated coverage of potential causal or risk factors, I will cite current available evidence as to the viability of the various factors that are presented. For protracted discussion, see Barkley (1990), Cantwell and Hanna (1989), Hynd et al. (1991), and Whalen (1989).

Genetic Factors. As noted above, a clear genetic anomaly has been found to associate specifically with ADHD (Hauser et al., 1993), but this primary causal agent is likely to account for only a tiny proportion of the many clinical cases of the disorder. For several decades investigators have utilized behavior genetic strategies to infer heritable, genetic contributions to hyperactivity or ADHD. Although early reports uncovered aggression, antisocial behavior, and substance abuse (i.e., antisocial-spectrum disorders) in biological relatives, these studies often confounded the children's inattentive/hyperactive behavior patterns with their aggression (e.g., Cantwell, 1975). In more recent investigations with adequate separation of these domains, the antisocial spectrum was found solely in the biological male relatives of ADHD children who also displayed comorbid aggressive-spectrum disorders themselves (Lahey, Piacentini, et al., 1988; Schachar & Wachsmuth, 1990). The only salient diagnostic category for relatives of nonaggressive ADHD children was a history of ADHD per se.

The careful family genetic investigations of Biederman and colleagues (e.g., Biederman, Munir, & Knee, 1987) suggest the possibility of differential genetic transmission for ADHD versus aggressive behavior patterns in children (see also Chapter 4). In fact, the twin studies of Goodman and Stevenson (1989a) and Stevenson (1992) indicate moderately strong heritabilities for attention deficits and hyperactivity in childhood, yet Plomin et al. (1990) summarized behavior genetic research on childhood aggression and found little, if any, evidence for their heritability.[7] Although convincing adoption studies have not yet been performed, the strong suggestion is that clinically significant ADHD symptomatology is partially heritable. Provocatively, behavioral genetic segregation analyses favor the contention that single gene transmission may be responsible for ADHD (Faraone, Biederman, Chen, et al., 1992). Yet environmental influences shape symptom expression (Goodman & Stevenson, 1989b).

What might be inherited to place a youngster at risk for ADHD symptomatology? For one thing, temperamental qualities of activity level and general "difficulty" are to some extent heritable (Plomin, 1986). Yet predictability from infant temperament to later behavior patterns is low without examining the adjoining influence of familial expectancies and reactions, meaning that interactive causal chains must be examined (Chess & Thomas, 1984; see subsequent section on family factors). Second, at a neurochemical level, evidence from known actions of successful pharmacologic treatments implicates the monoamines dopamine, norepinephrine, and epinephrine and the indoleamine serotonin as mediating neurotransmitters (Zametkin & Rapoport, 1987). Our knowledge base regarding neurotransmission is still rudimentary, however; furthermore, it is dangerous to reason backward from known actions of treatments to etiologic factors. For example, successful treatment with behavioral therapy does not implicate a lack of reinforcement as a causal factor in the genesis of the disorder; pharmacologic agents may "work" at levels of neurochemistry and neuroanatomy that are many steps removed from primary causal influences. In addition, the central nervous system is constructed in complex fashion, so that theories implicating single neurotransmitter pathology are bound to be overly simplistic.

Despite a massive failure to replicate key laboratory findings with respect to psychobiologic influences on attention deficits and hyperactivity (Zametkin & Rapoport, 1987), active theorizing and research continues. With respect to the pathophysiology of ADHD, McCracken (1991) provides evidence consistent with a central role for dopamine in the ventral tegmental areas of the brain as well as for norepinephrine and epinephrine in the locus coeruleus. Furthermore, in a groundbreaking study with adults who revealed histories consistent with criteria for ADHD, Zametkin et al. (1990) found evidence for reduced efficiency of glucose metabolism in the prefrontal cortex and motor cortical areas. Interest in the role of prefrontal structures that subserve the development of response inhibition continues as well (Barkley, in press). Despite the excitement generated by such biological findings and theorizing, it must be kept in mind that (a) environmental, as well as genetic factors, may be responsible for individual differences in the above-noted biological features; and (b) the field has far to go before linkages between clearly explicated genetic transmission and actual neural pathology pertinent to ADHD are forged.

Congenital Factors. Retrospective accounts suggest that a host of congenital factors may be related to ADHD symptomatology, including prenatal difficulties, low birth weight, diseases of infancy, and early neurologic insult (see review in Cantwell & Hanna, 1989). Although there is undoubtedly sensitivity in the prediction of later ADHD from such events, there is no compelling evidence for specificity in such predictions. That is, such perinatal and congenital factors may predispose to a range of later child psychopathology. Still, the assessor must be sensitive to reports of these types of risks in obtaining a developmental history from the family (see Chapter 2).

Although family environment will be discussed in more detail subsequently, findings from the Kauai study of Werner and colleagues deserve reiteration. In this prospective population investigation, environmental influences and quality of caretaking outweighed such congenital factors as perinatal stress and low birth weight in predicting adaptive functioning in later life (Werner & Smith, 1977). Early biological difficulties exist in a complex matrix of psychosocial influences; interactions between the two are of crucial importance for shaping symptomatology and resilience.

Considerable public awareness has been generated in recent years regarding the effects of maternal substance use during pregnancy. Whereas high levels of drinking during critical periods may yield the full spectrum of fetal alcohol syndrome (FAS), which includes mental retardation, there is strong suspicion that somewhat lower levels of drinking may induce the kinds of disinhibition, learning difficulties, and behavioral disruption characteristic of ADHD (Brown, Coles, Platzman, & Hill, 1993). Other teratogenic substances, like cocaine and even nicotine (Nichols & Chen, 1981), may also be culprits for ADHD-related symptomatology. Children growing up in such homes are also likely to be exposed to discord and disorganization; teasing apart early neurologic insults from chronic psychosocial deprivation and disruption is virtually impossible.

Toxins and Environmental Agents. The roles of diet and of possible allergic reactions in the genesis and expression of ADHD are controversial. Although some well-reasoned arguments favor further exploration of allergic mechanisms in ADHD symptomatology, recent evidence from a population-wide investigation failed to confirm any relationship between allergic manifestations and ADHD (McGee, Stanton, & Sears, 1993). As for dietary factors, the available evidence does not strongly support the role of food additives in ADHD (Conners, 1980; Kavale & Forness, 1983), and the lack of any causal role of sugar in hyperactive behavior has been conclusively demonstrated (Milich, Wolraich, & Lindgren, 1986). On the other hand, exposure to lead, even at levels that fall short of clinical toxicity, is associated with small but robust decrements in intellectual performance and with distractible, impulsive school behavior. Recent prospective research (Fergusson, Horwood, & Lynskey, 1993; Needleman, Schell, Bellinger, Leviton, & Allred, 1990) reveals a longitudinal linkage between elevated lead levels in childhood and impaired behavior and cognitive performance in adolescence, even with potential confounding factors controlled. Once again, however, the specificity of such associations to clinical ADHD is indeterminate.

Familial Risk Factors or Causal Agents. In Chapter 1, I presented a brief historical account of the field's conceptions of the role of familial factors in determining ADHD symptomatology. Over the years, the Zeitgeist has alternated between psychodynamic or family-systemic conceptions implicating parent-child interactions as primary causes and specific biological explanations. More currently, interactive and transactional models that examine interrelations between the child's psychobiologic tendencies and the family, school, and neighborhood environment have risen to ascendancy.

Perhaps the most prevalent viewpoint in the field is that of "goodness of fit" (Chess & Thomas, 1984). Given that certain young children are temperamentally predisposed to high activity levels and low regularity in bodily functions, the critical question is how parents or caretakers respond. In exemplary developmental research, toddlers' exploration of the environment was completely determined by the interaction of temperamental style with type of caretaking, such that highly active infants confronted with stimulating parenting as well as low-activity infants met by understimulating parents displayed similarly low exploration rates (Gandour, 1989). On the other hand, the converse "matches" produced high levels of exploration. In short, it is perhaps the case that neither the infant's psychobiological tendencies nor the caretakers' attitudes and behaviors alone but rather the interaction of the two that shapes behavioral content and style.

It is easy to imagine, for example, that an inordinately fussy and active infant would strain all but the most resilient parents. Similarly, a disorganized family setting could promote and perpetuate initially mild levels of child activity and impulsivity. Clearly needed are long-term prospective investigations that can examine the joint effects of family style and child predispositions.

If they are not primary causal factors, can negative parent-child interactions account for the maintenance or escalation of externalizing behavior patterns in youngsters with ADHD symptomatology? Two recent reports indicate just such a role for negative, coercive parenting in preschool (Campbell et al., 1991) and elementary-school-aged (Anderson et al., in press) youngsters. Specifically, the degree of maternal harshness and coercion in parent-child interactions predicted concurrent or subsequent noncompliance, hyperactivity, and antisocial behavior in these samples, even when initial indices of the child's externalizing behavior were controlled. Indeed, a large literature exists that implicates disharmonious familial interaction in the genesis of frank aggression (Hetherington & Martin, 1986; Patterson, 1982). Given the central importance of comorbid aggression for ADHD (see Chapter 4), understanding of familial interactions is of central importance for prediction and intervention.

I noted in Chapter 1 that recent work of Jacobvitz and Sroufe (1987) has implicated overstimulating mother-child interactions early in life as a primary causal factor for ADHD in impoverished inner-city families. Even with statistical control of early biological child variables, a pattern of intrusive caregiving predicted dimensional and categorical ADHD several years later. This research has an interesting parallel in recent work from Puerto Rico by Bauermeister et al. (1992), who found that impulsive-hyperactive behavior characterized a cluster of low-income youngsters for whom familial interactions may have been the instigating factor.

Yet implicating such psychosocial factors as primary causes is fraught with difficulty. For example, the primarily teenaged mothers in the sample of Jacobvitz and Sroufe (1987) may themselves have been impulsive. Such impulsivity, which could have contributed to their risk for early pregnancy and their tendency to overstimulate their children, may have been transmitted via heritable as well as psychosocial means. In short, the development of most cases of ADHD is more likely to constitute a complex intertwining of intraindividual, familial, and broader systems factors than a purely environmental or purely genetic causal route (see

Chapter 5). The possibility of psychosocial origins of some types of ADHD behavior among lower-SES individuals is intriguing, however, inviting the notion of equifinality: namely, that substantially different causal pathways may lead to similar behavior patterns (see Cicchetti & Richters, 1993).

SUMMARY

Overlap across genetic, congenital, and familial categories of etiologic risk is probably the rule rather than the exception for explanations of ADHD. Recent evidence implicates a specific genetic cause for a small group of diagnosed youngsters, revealing the importance of further exploration of psychobiologic risk factors and causal agents. In addition, moderate heritability has been found for symptom patterns of inattention and hyperactivity, but substantial room still exists for environmental influence in most cases. A host of perinatal influences may influence later behavior patterns that are related to ADHD, yet the specificity of such factors is indeterminate, and quality of caretaking appears to outweigh perinatal difficulties in mediating outcome. Toxic factors (ingestion of lead) may be pertinent to ADHD symptomatology in some youngsters, but allergic or food-related hypotheses have received less support. Discordant familial interchanges appear to be a maintaining or escalating factor in families with a child displaying ADHD behavior patterns; such familial interaction styles are particularly linked with comorbid aggression and antisocial behavior. Although attachment-oriented research has recently implicated overstimulating parenting as a key cause of ADHD for low-income youngsters, interactive models incorporating psychobiologic and familial factors are likely to provide more explanatory power. Perhaps the most salient theme from this discussion is that ADHD symptomatology is multidetermined and that substantially different etiologic paths may contribute to similar behavior patterns in different subgroups. In the next chapter, I specifically tackle the issue of the multiplicity of subgroups that may be diagnosed as having clinically significant attention deficits and hyperactivity.

NOTES

1. Sometimes methodologic difficulties are compounded in research investigations. For instance, a cross-sectional study of the causal role of family interaction patterns in

hyperactive behavior may fail to employ assessment strategies that differentiate ADHD from aggression. In this case, any discovery that the "hyperactive" sample displays inconsistent, harsh family discipline may be attributed to ADHD rather than to the children's aggressive status. Furthermore, in this case the lack of a prospective design prevents attribution of a causal role to the family factors.

2. Given the difficulties inherent in ascertaining convergence across various sources of assessment information—lab measures, objective observations, teacher ratings, self-reports—the optimal means of ascertaining a potential disorder's validity is to observe its divergence from other disorders on the basis of external factors like family history, course, treatment response, and concurrent correlates (see Chapter 1). Such "external" validity is believed to be more important than the internal coherence among constituent measures in establishing the disorder's viability, particularly given low representativeness of any single measure of the disorder.

3. The analysis of Douglas (1983) also implicates dysregulation of arousal systems, with specific levels of arousal at any given moment determined by particular task parameters. Douglas' work is exemplary for its integration of potential neural mechanisms as they interact with shifting environmental circumstances. I should point out, as well, that the neurological underpinnings of arousal and attention are exceedingly complex, leading to speculation of deficits in multiple neural loci (Voeller, 1991).

4. Recent family genetic data of Faraone et al. (in press-a) also implicate single gene transmission of ADHD. Single-locus genetic hypotheses are likely to receive close scrutiny and attempts at replication in the years to come. Such modes of transmission, however, need not imply that the presence of the gene inevitably signals the disorder; environmental factors may mitigate symptom expression (Goodman & Stevenson, 1989b).

5. Nongenetic biological factors (e.g., low birth weight) may also shape the developing infant and toddler's ability to interact with the environment, further exemplifying the intertwining of biological and environmental contributions to causation. In the case of teratogenic influences (i.e., those caused by intrauterine exposure to drugs), the mother's ingestion of substances and their subsequent filtration into the fetal amniotic environment can induce structural biological changes in the developing nervous system. Here, the immediate causal factor is simultaneously environmental and biological. Furthermore, the mother's risk for substance abuse may relate to both environmental stressors and, in some cases, biological predisposition for a substance abuse pattern. Our thinking and language are inadequate for handling such complex, intertwined causal factors.

6. It is also quite helpful to understand how many noncases failed to show the risk factor (specificity) and how many of those individuals without the causal agent went on to become noncases (negative predictive power). Milich, Widiger, and Landau (1987) provide an extremely illuminating example of the use of these statistics to inform the field about the utility of various symptom patterns for establishing a diagnosis of ADHD.

7. Two additional points from genetic research regarding aggression and antisocial behavior are salient. First, despite the weak findings regarding the heritability of dimensions of aggressive behavior in childhood (Plomin et al., 1990), somewhat stronger evidence exists for the heritability of persistent adolescent and adult criminality, revealing the need to differentiate subgroups of aggressive/antisocial children (see Moffitt, in press). Second, whereas nonshared environmental influences are important for most manifestations of child psychopathology, there are great similarities in within-family influence on aggression and antisocial behavior (Plomin et al., 1990). Thus familial environments may be of particular pertinence for understanding aggression in ADHD youngsters (see below).

4

SUBGROUPS AND COMORBIDITY

A persistent theme throughout the previous chapters has been the diversity and heterogeneity of the clinical syndrome of ADHD in childhood. I now discuss several attempts at subgrouping children with clinically significant attention deficits and hyperactivity, beginning with the concept of pervasive versus situational variants of the syndrome and then moving to attention deficit disorder with and without accompanying hyperactivity. Next, in considering the linkages between ADHD and comorbid childhood diagnoses—particularly aggressive-spectrum disorders, learning disabilities, and internalizing disorders—I examine the value of considering ADHD youngsters with and without such associated conditions as distinct subgroups. Finally, I discuss the critically important population of girls with ADHD, considering whether females with this diagnosis display a fundamentally similar or different symptom pattern. My overall goal is to examine critically the value of subtyping the large array of children who become diagnosed with ADHD, with specific focus on whether more homogeneous subcategories yield greater specificity regarding etiology, core features, key correlates, and response to intervention.

PERVASIVE VERSUS SITUATIONAL HYPERACTIVITY

For many years British investigators have contended that a diagnosis of hyperkinesis (to use the preferred term in the United Kingdom) involves severe levels of impulsivity, inattention, and particularly hyperactivity as judged by both parents and teachers and as noticed in clinic settings as well.[1] The contention is that only such pervasively hyperactive (or hyperkinetic) youngsters truly comprise a clinical syndrome in terms of intellectual, academic, and interpersonal deficits as well as negative course (e.g., Schachar, Rutter, & Smith, 1981). In fact, Schachar (1991) contends that pervasively hyperactive youngsters form a qualitatively distinct group from so-called situationally hyperactive children (i.e., those identified by only one source). The pervasive group has a relatively low prevalence rate of approximately 1% (Sandoval et al., 1980; Schachar, 1991) and shows evidence of clear neurodevelopmental delay, as evidenced by speech and language deficits, motoric clumsiness, lowered IQ scores, and perinatal complications. The contention with regard to situationally hyperactive children is that they are not as clearly distinguishable from nondiagnosed youngsters and that they may, in some cases, be defined largely on the basis of parental intolerance or transitory environmental events. In short, this group may not comprise a valid disorder (Schachar, 1991).

Yet several key methodologic issues and empirical findings cloud the separability of pervasive from situational hyperactivity and the interpretation that only pervasive hyperactivity is related to impairment. First, Biederman, Keenan, and Faraone (1990) found that despite the modest associations of parent and teacher informants with respect to ratings of child problem behavior (see Achenbach et al., 1987), parent identification of ADHD youngsters using *DSM-III-R* criteria predicted, with 90% accuracy, teacher identification of the same sample. Thus a carefully chosen sample on the basis of parent ratings may overwhelmingly yield a sample that also displays school dysfunction; almost all of a well-defined "situational" group of ADHD youngsters may display pervasive symptomatology. Clinically, it is important to obtain information about school behavior and performance from the parent, particularly if direct assessments from the teacher are not available.

Second, in some research investigations, situational groups of hyperactive children are formed by combining solely parent-identified and solely teacher-identified ADHD youngsters into an overall group of children who have been identified by one source only. Yet because of the clear differences between groups identified by different sources, such a "combined situational" group may be problematic. Costello, Loeber, and Stouthamer-Loeber (1991) found that although an omnibus situational sample appeared to be less disturbed than a pervasively hyperactive group, the teacher-identified situational youngsters were just as deviant as pervasively hyperactive children with respect to school measures, and parent-identified situational children were equivalent to the pervasive children regarding home variables. Furthermore, as for such objective indicators as IQ scores, special education placement, and repeating a grade, the parent-identified, teacher-identified, and pervasive groups did not differ. In other words, lumping ADHD youngsters identified by a single-source into a global "situational" group may mask key differences that relate to the source of diagnosis. Along similar lines, in a study reported by Klein and Mannuzza (1991), teacher-identified ADHD youngsters displayed long-term risk for continuing psychiatric problems that was comparable to the risk incurred by pervasively hyperactive youngsters, but children identified only by parents displayed much more favorable long-term outcomes. Such findings mandate that careful attention be paid to the precise source of identification of situationally hyperactive youngsters.

Third, with data from the Ontario Child Health Study, Szatmari, Boyle, and Offord (1989) concluded that single-source-identified (i.e., situational) ADHD was associated with marked impairment. That is, such youngsters displayed high rates of peer problems, poor physical health, and general skill deficits as well as a history of developmental delays. At least in this report, a diagnosis of pervasive hyperactivity was not necessary to yield a clinically impaired sample.

As can be seen, evidence regarding the similarity of ADHD youngsters identified by single versus multiple sources is contradictory. It does appear that requiring symptom presence in two or more settings increases the diagnostic threshold, serving to reduce the prevalence rate and ensuring a more disturbed sample. Such a goal may be desirable to be sure that ADHD is not overdiagnosed and that treatments are not overapplied. Furthermore, there is less doubt about the severity of impairment for children independently identified in both school and home settings. As noted earlier, *DSM-IV* has departed from past American diagnostic practice by tentatively adopting a criterion that requires dysfunction in two or more settings for ascertaining a diagnosis of ADHD.[2] The possible downside to such a requirement is that some children with significant school problems (but not home-based difficulties) will fail to meet criteria, possibly denying needed interventions to children showing clear impairment and long-term risk for negative outcome. A cost-benefit analysis regarding the pros and cons of more versus less stringent diagnostic criteria for ADHD presents a worthy challenge to subsequent investigators.

ATTENTION DEFICIT DISORDER
WITH AND WITHOUT HYPERACTIVITY

As discussed in Chapter 1, major changes in terminology and diagnostic criteria were evidenced with the advent of *DSM-III* in 1980. The core syndrome, termed attention deficit disorder (ADD), was defined by significant problems in inattention and impulsivity; if meaningful difficulties with motor overactivity were also exhibited, a diagnosis of attention deficit disorder with hyperactivity (ADDH) was assigned. Although some research on the distinction between these subtypes had begun to appear by the mid-1980s (e.g., Lahey, Schaughency, Hynd, Carlson, & Nieves, 1987), such investigations were not considered sufficient to continue the distinction, and the criteria for ADHD shifted in *DSM-III-R* to a polythetic mix of 14 symptoms involving inattention, impulsivity, and hyperactivity (American Psychiatric Association, 1987). "Pure" ADD (or what is sometimes called ADD/WO, signifying ADD without hyperactivity) was relegated to a category termed *undifferentiated ADD* that lacked operational criteria. An upshot of this diagnostic scheme was to blur important distinctions between youngsters presenting primarily with symptoms of poor concentration and cognitive disorganization versus those with additional problems of impulse control and motoric overactivity. (Note that, to standardize terminology across various studies, I will designate attention deficits without accompanying hyperactivity as *ADD/WO* and attention deficits plus hyperactivity as *ADD/H*.)

Research clarifying the differences between ADD/WO and ADD/H subgroups has continued to build over the years. The overwhelming conclusion is that these subcategories clearly comprise distinct entities; as noted earlier, *DSM-IV* will feature an inattentive subtype of ADHD, to be distinguished from a primarily hyperactive-impulsive subcategory and a group composed of children with both types of symptom patterns.[3] I now briefly summarize evidence for this distinction and speculate as to the nature of children who display ADD/WO. Only a few of the large number of individual investigations of both clinic-based and community samples will be cited individually; systematic and cogent reviews of the literature are available in Cantwell and Baker (1992), Carlson (1986), Goodyear and Hynd (1992), and Lahey and Carlson (1991).

First, do subgroups of children conforming to ADD/WO versus ADD/H patterns exist clinically? In the cluster analytic research of Lahey, Pelham et al. (1988) and Hart et al. (1993), described briefly in Chapter 3, a distinct group of children with deficits solely in inattention/

disorganization emerged, complementing a larger group containing children with deficits in inattention/disorganization plus impulsivity/hyperactivity. Thus not only do two core dimensions pertinent to the domain of interest appear in factor analytic investigations, but distinguishable clusters of children corresponding to ADD/WO versus ADD/H patterns emerge in careful cluster analytic investigations. Furthermore these clusters corresponded closely to clinical diagnoses that separated ADD youngsters with and without hyperactivity (Lahey et al., 1988; Hart et al., 1993). The mere presence of such groups in cluster analytic research, however, does not attest to their separability with respect to key criterion variables related to family history, pathophysiology, peer relations, cognitive functioning, course, and treatment response. Is there evidence for such divergent validity?

Table 4.1 presents a summation of key differences between groups defined as ADD/WO versus those characterized as having ADD with hyperactivity (ADD/H). As aptly discussed by Goodyear and Hynd (1992), many results of pertinent investigations are difficult to compare, in that diagnostic decision rules for differentiating these two putative subgroups have varied greatly across different reports. Nonetheless, several key themes have emerged.

Regarding family history, Barkley, DuPaul, and McMurray (1990) provide evidence for the presence of externalizing spectrum disorders in the mothers and fathers of ADD/H youngsters, with internalizing disorders and learning disabilities characterizing biological relatives of ADD/WO children. As for comorbid symptom patterns in the youngsters themselves, the ADD/WO group strongly tends to display significantly fewer indicators of aggressive or conduct-disordered behavior than does the ADD/H group. The latter category is more likely to have received comorbid diagnoses of ODD or CD (Goodyear & Hynd, 1992), as well as more frequent school suspensions and placements in special education, both of which are frequently related to externalizing behavior patterns (Barkley, DuPaul, & McMurray, 1990). In addition, there is some evidence that the ADD/WO group displays a preponderance of internalizing symptomatology. Importantly, the attentional deficits displayed by the two groups appear to differ. That is, children diagnosed as having ADD/WO tend to be characterized as sluggish, forgetful, drowsy, apathetic, and prone to daydreaming, whereas the inattentive/hyperactive or combined group displays the more classic signs of disorganization, need for close supervision, failure to complete tasks, and the like.

TABLE 4.1 Differences Between Attention Deficit Disorder Without Hyperactivity (ADD/WO) and Attention Deficit Disorder With Hyperactivity (ADD/H)

Feature	ADD/WO	ADD/H
Family history of psychopathology	Internalizing-spectrum disorders; learning disabilities	Antisocial-spectrum disorders and ADHD
Symptomatology	Distinct pattern of attention problems (sluggish, daydreaming; some evidence for internalizing problems)	Oppositional and aggressive behaviors
Peer problems	Social isolation, peer neglect	Active peer rejection
Academic achievement	Some evidence for higher rates of learning disabilities	Higher rates of school suspension and special education placement
Neuropsychological deficits	Suggestion of slow automatization, similar to children with learning disabilities	Mixed evidence for frontal/prefrontal deficits
Course	Few extant data	Risk for antisocial outcomes and negative course; disinhibitory behaviors are predictors
Treatment response	Tend to respond to lower stimulant dosages	Tend to respond to moderate stimulant dosages

The difference in the cognitive and attentional problems displayed by the two groups may be qualitative and not just quantitative.

As for peer relations, both groups tend to be disliked by peers, but at least some evidence suggests that ADD/WO is marked more by social withdrawal and neglect from age-mates, whereas the combined group receives frank peer rejection. Given the role of comorbid aggression in mediating peer disapprobation (Erhardt & Hinshaw, 1993), such a result is hardly surprising. I must note, along this line, that even among ADD children of both subcategories who do not display comorbid diagnoses, significant peer relationship problems exist (Carlson, Lahey, Frame, Walker, & Hynd, 1987). Thus such difficulties are linked with the core problems of ADHD and are not simply related to associated diagnoses.

Regarding academic underachievement, the picture is again mixed: Some reports find that both subgroups display equivalent levels of academic impairment, but other reports suggest a preponderance of specific learning disabilities among ADD/WO youth (Hynd et al., 1991). The conclusion of Hynd et al. (1991) is that ADD/WO is a disorder of attention and cognition with significant implications for major underachievement, whereas the nonspecific academic problems of the ADD/H subgroup are related more to impulsivity and disinhibition. With respect to neuropsychological and neurobiological findings, the careful review of Goodyear and Hynd (1992) indicates that, regarding the development of automatic processing skills, children in the ADD/WO subgroup show the same pattern of deficits as do learning-disabled youngsters, differentiating them from ADD/H youngsters. Electrophysiologic indicators, however, are inconsistent in separating subgroups, despite the consistent findings that all children with attention deficits and/or hyperactivity differ from comparison children.

What of the key outcome domains of long-term course and treatment response? Although data are sparse, Fischer, Barkley, Edelbrock, and Smallish (in press) have recently concluded that impulsivity/hyperactivity is a stronger predictor of negative adolescent outcome than is inattention per se; such data suggest subgroup differences in prognosis. In addition, Barkley, DuPaul, and McMurray (1990) administered dose-response trials of stimulant medications to carefully diagnosed groups of ADD/WO versus ADD/H youngsters, finding that differences in outcome on key dependent measures did not differ across the groups. A greater percentage of the ADD/WO group, however, showed a negative response to medication, and on the average they displayed optimal responses to lower dosage levels. Thus quantitative (if not qualitative) differences in medication response were observed (see also Chapter 6).

In sum, considerable evidence supports the differential validity of subgroups of attention deficit disordered youngsters differing with respect to the disinhibitory processes of behavioral impulsivity and hyperactivity (see Table 4.1). Whereas two distinct syndromes cannot conclusively be supported on the basis of available evidence (Goodyear & Hynd, 1992), a prevalent belief is that ADD/WO actually resembles an internalizing more than an externalizing disorder, given its (a) characteristic slow cognitive tempo and drowsy, daydreaming features; (b) risk of incurring social withdrawal and peer neglect; (c) different pattern of family history; and (d) greater likelihood of adverse response to stimulant medications (see Pliszka, 1989, for similar findings regarding the stimulant response of ADHD youngsters with comorbid anxiety disorders). Overall, combining these two subcategories into an omnibus cluster of children with "ADHD" (as was done with *DSM-III-R*) may result in a loss of crucial information.[4]

COMORBID AGGRESSION
IN CHILDREN WITH ADHD

In recent years the field has increasingly accepted the partial independence of ADHD-related symptomatology on the one hand and aggression/conduct problems on the other (Hinshaw, 1987b; Loney, 1987). Substantially different family histories, cognitive patterns, concurrent measures of family climate and parenting style, and (perhaps) genetic/biological vulnerabilities exist for the separate disorders (see also Chapter 3). There is little doubt, however, that (a) dimensions of these domains are moderately to substantially correlated (Fergusson, Horwood, & Lloyd, 1991), and (b) categorical ADHD occurs jointly with ODD or CD occur at rates that are far greater than chance (Biederman, Newcorn, & Sprich, 1991; Hinshaw, 1987b). Indeed, rates of comorbidity range from 30% to over 50% in both clinic-referred and community samples. The purpose of this section is to examine the characteristics of this comorbid subgroup, with the goal of ascertaining the unique features of children who display concurrent ADHD and aggressive-spectrum disorders.[5]

First, in an examination of conduct-disordered children with or without accompanying ADHD, Walker, Lahey, Hynd, and Frame (1987) noted the marked severity of the jointly diagnosed subgroup with respect to associated features. Importantly, such features were unique to the overlap of CD with ADHD and not to its comorbidity with comparably severe levels of internalizing disorders. Thus there appears to be a distinctive and specific pattern of dysfunction associated with the subgroup displaying comorbid ADHD and CD. Such findings were amplified, from a slightly different perspective, by Szatmari, Boyle, and Offord (1989). These investigators concluded that a comorbid ADHD plus CD subgroup showed the impairing features of both single conditions (i.e., the developmental delays of ADHD youngsters and the psychosocial disadvantage of the CD youth) but in a different configuration than would be expected by a simple addition of the single disorders. In other words, the comorbid group was a true hybrid. Furthermore, in an extensive investigation of family history patterns, Faraone, Biederman, Keenan, and Tsuang (1991b) found evidence compatible with the conclusion that ADHDs with and without comorbid disruptive behavior disorders are etiologically distinct with respect to familial transmission. Although interpretations of the complex findings defy simple description, the implication is that the comorbid subgroup may be qualitatively distinct from the single disorders.[6]

Just what are the uniquely difficult characteristics of this overlapping subgroup? For one thing, despite inconsistent findings, some reports contend that ADHD-aggressive youngsters are more likely to display severe patterns of underachievement than is either single-disorder subgroup (see review in Hinshaw, 1992b). Next, whereas peer relationship problems plague nearly all youngsters with ADHD, rates of peer rejection are nearly universal for ADHD children who also display additional disruptive behavior disorders (Milich & Landau, 1989). Third, and crucially, the long-term course of children displaying both patterns of disorder in childhood appears to be particularly grim (see Chapter 5 for elaboration of the developmental trajectories of each symptom domain). Fourth, suggestive evidence exists that although qualitatively different response patterns to pharmacologic treatment regimens do not seem likely (Barkley, McMurray, Edelbrock, & Robbins, 1989; Klorman et al., 1988), the overlapping subgroup is particularly refractory to psychosocial treatment packages that are currently in use (for a review, see Hinshaw & Erhardt, 1991). Milich and Landau (1989) cogently summarize the body of research regarding these jointly impaired children, contending that (a) the skill deficits related to ADHD render them relatively unable to perform key developmental tasks and (b) the defiance characteristic of aggressive-spectrum disorders depletes motivation and effort. This multiple loading of skill deficits, defiant attitudes, and poor motivation depicts the intractibility of such a subgroup.

Given the evidence reported in Chapter 3 for moderately strong heritabilities for ADHD behavior patterns, along with the quite equivocal evidence for such transmission regarding childhood aggression (Plomin et al., 1990), it is tempting to speculate, with respect to the comorbid subgroup, that genetic/biological risk for ADHD is compounded by deviant, coercive parent-child interactions to yield concurrent aggression. Such a simplified risk model, however, ignores the potential for familial factors to contribute to ADHD symptomatology (Campbell et al., 1991) and for biological factors, whether genetic or congenital (Mednick, Brennan, & Kandel, 1988), to play key roles for at least some subgroups of persistently aggressive youth (see also Moffitt, 1993). Furthermore, active transactions across biological and psychosocial factors are likely to be operative in the developmental trajectories of youngsters with comorbid ADHD and aggression (Moffitt, 1990; see also Chapter 5). In all, given the severity and potential distinctiveness of their symptomatology and course, the comorbid subgroup of children with concurrent ADHD and aggression is likely to command considerable attention with respect to both research efforts and intervention trials.

ASSOCIATED LEARNING DISABILITIES
AND UNDERACHIEVEMENT

I noted previously that various forms of underachievement are quite likely to accompany ADHD but that formal learning disabilities—defined as marked disparities between obtained achievement in academic subjects and intelligence as measured by individual IQ tests—are rarer. Still, learning disabilities are comorbid with ADHD at rates well above chance, with recent figures ranging from less than 10% to approximately 25% (Hinshaw, 1992b; Semrud-Clikeman et al., 1992). Furthermore, recent evidence reveals that the neuropsychological underpinnings of learning disabilities in youngsters with comorbid ADHD are transmitted somewhat independently of the behavioral manifestations of ADHD per se (Faraone, Biederman, Krifcher, et al., 1992). The issue to receive brief attention here is whether the combination of these two syndromes comprises a unique subgroup.

The answer to this question is difficult to determine. Research from the past decade (Halperin, Gittelman, Klein, & Rudel, 1984) failed to find substantial distinctiveness between ADHD youngsters with and without diagnosed reading disabilities with respect to behavioral or demographic factors. On the other hand, exploration of intervention studies reveals that the kinds of treatment that yield important short-term gains for youngsters with ADHD—like stimulant medications—do not lead to fundamental improvements in underlying reading disabilities (Gittelman, Klein, & Feingold, 1983). The benefits for learning and cognition that do accrue to stimulant treatment appear to be related to nonspecific enhancement of attention rather than to any specific amelioration of phonologic processing (Balthazor, Wagner, & Pelham, 1991). Thus, for the comorbid subgroup with both ADHD and learning disabilities, interventions specific to each problem domain must be supplied (Hinshaw, 1992a; see also Chapter 6). In short, whereas the general problems with school performance that pertain to the majority of children with ADHD may be aided by interventions that improve impulsivity, attention span, and behavioral organization, the presence of specific learning disabilities mandates specific educational interventions tailored to the achievement deficits. To that extent, assessment of comorbid learning disabilities is a priority, and the overlapping subgroup bears separate consideration.

COMORBID ANXIETY DISORDERS AND DEPRESSION

In recent years consensus has emerged that ADHD displays above-chance comorbidity with the internalizing spectrum of anxiety disorders. As summarized by Biederman, Newcorn, and Sprich (1991), the rate of overlap with such manifestations as overanxious disorder, separation anxiety, and phobic disorders is in the neighborhood of 25%. As discussed in the earlier section on attention deficit disorders with and without hyperactivity, some investigations have found a greater likelihood of comorbidity with anxiety disorders or social withdrawal for ADD/WO than for ADD/H. Although the familial investigation of Biederman, Faraone, Keenan, Steingard, and Tsuang (1991) suggests that ADHD and anxiety disorders are not etiologically independent, their results render indeterminate whether the comorbid subgroup is independent of ADHD per se or whether familial etiologic factors are shared between ADHD youngsters with and without accompanying anxiety disorders.

What are the treatment implications, if any, for children with the comorbid conditions? The research of Pliszka (1989) has been influential in its determination that ADHD children who also display anxiety disorders are markedly less likely to respond favorably to stimulant medications than are ADHD youngsters without such comorbidity. In this report, the comorbid subgroup was more likely to display a positive placebo response, cutting down on their rates of improvement from actual medication. Given that extremely few predictors of response to medication treatment have emerged in the field (see Chapter 6), the finding of reduced treatment responsiveness in children with overlapping ADHD and anxiety disorders is of clinical and potentially of theoretical importance.

Considerably more controversy exists with regard to the comorbidity of affective or mood disorders with ADHD. As reviewed by Biederman, Newcorn, and Sprich (1991), overlap rates have been reported to range from chance levels to over 70% in various reports. A number of influential investigators have not found enhanced risk for mood disorders in youngsters with ADHD, either contemporaneously or at long-term follow-up (Gittelman et al., 1985; Lahey, Pelham, et al., 1988). Yet in other reports with both community and clinic samples, overlap has been found to occur (e.g., J. C. Anderson et al., 1987; Biederman, Faraone, Keenan, & Tsuang, 1991). Such widely disparate estimates of comorbidity are puzzling.

Resolution of these discrepant findings will be important for several reasons. First, given the known comorbidity between CD and major mood disorders in children and adolescence, along with the clearly established linkages between CD and ADHD, clarification of possible developmental progressions from ADHD to both aggressive-spectrum and mood disorders would be important. Second, given the suggestion that children with comorbid ADHD and mood disorders may respond preferentially to antidepressant as opposed to stimulant medication (Pliszka, 1987), accurate diagnostic evaluation is in order. Yet a positive response to antidepressant treatment in a youngster with ADHD does not specify an underlying mood disorder, because ADHD youngsters without evidence of comorbidity may show beneficial effects. (Furthermore, no controlled data exist to support the efficacy of antidepressant medications for major depression in childhood.) Finally, another in the series of familial risk articles by Biederman and colleagues suggests that youngsters with ADHD and mood disorders share common familial risk factors, with the possibility that psychosocial variables promote the expression of comorbidity (Biederman, Faraone, Keenan, & Tsuang, 1991). Again, however, such data were generated by a research team that typically yields high rates of comorbidity of ADHD and mood disorders; the generalizability of the findings remains to be established. In short, this area is likely to generate controversy and further research over the coming years.

GIRLS WITH ADHD

Although not comprising a subgroup of the kinds discussed in the previous portions of this chapter, females with ADHD are an understudied population who have been hypothesized to differ in key ways from boys exhibiting this symptom pattern. Specifically, given the preponderance of boys with ADHD among clinic-referred populations —the male:female disparity among clinic attendees may be as high as 8:1 or 10:1—and the less prominent but still salient overrepresentation of boys among community samples (Szatmari, Offord, & Boyle, 1989), it may be that females require a more severe biological predisposition to cross the threshold into diagnosis (Cloninger, Christiansen, Reich, & Gottesman, 1978).[7] Alternatively, it may be that males show more variability in symptom expression (James & Taylor, 1990) or that they are more likely to display comorbidity with other disruptive behavior disorders, fueling their disproportionate rates of referral. What is the profile of girls who display ADHD, and what mechanisms may contribute to their lower prevalence rates?

Relatively few systematic reports have appeared. Because of the relative paucity of diagnosed girls in clinic studies, many investigators choose to study only boys with the disorder, perpetuating the belief that the condition is important only in males (McGee & Feehan, 1991). Several key investigations, in fact, reveal fundamental similarities regarding manifestations of psychopathology and of parent-child interactions in boys and girls with ADHD (e.g., Befera & Barkley, 1985). In addition, family histories of psychopathology have been shown to be strikingly similar in males and females with carefully ascertained diagnoses (Faraone, Biederman, Keenan, & Tsuang, 1991a). Furthermore, well-controlled studies reveal a fundamental similarity in response profile to stimulant medications across genders (Pelham, Walker, Sturges, & Hoza, 1989). The bulk of such evidence supports the contention that the disorders appear quite similar in boys and girls.

Yet, in some reports, meaningful differences have also received support. Most saliently, (a) boys display greater levels of aggressive and antisocial behaviors (Berry, Shaywitz, & Shaywitz, 1985); and (b) diagnosed girls tend to display higher rates of cognitive impairment, language dysfunction, and compromised neurological status (Berry et al., 1985; James & Taylor, 1990). The investigations revealing such differences have tended to sample from clinic populations, perhaps indicating that any gender differences pertain largely to referral biases. Yet in an epidemiologic investigation in Canada, Szatmari, Boyle, and Offord (1989) found clear gender differences regarding comorbidity with conduct disorder, leading them to conclude that, for girls, ADHD may be a form of CD. Other population surveys, however, support the fundamental similarity of ADHD in boys and girls (McGee, Williams, & Silva, 1987). At this point, the safest conclusion may be that although marked differences in the expression of the disorder do not seem to characterize females, comorbid aggressive-spectrum disorders predominate in boys, and tantalizing evidence suggests the possibility of more severe cognitive, learning, and language deficits in the female group. James and Taylor (1990) hypothesize that—at least with respect to hyperkinesis as opposed to ADHD—boys may develop symptoms via similar mechanisms to those responsible for normal variation in attention, impulsivity, and overactivity, whereas for girls organic factors may be more salient. Further data will be critical to help resolve these issues.

In a provocative review, McGee and Feehan (1991) have raised the issue of the potential for underrecognition and underreporting of females with symptoms characteristic of ADHD. Specifically, because teacher ratings, but not parent ratings, show disproportionate levels of hyperactive and impulsive behaviors in boys, it may be that teachers fail to recognize inattentive behavior patterns unless they are also accompanied by disruptive behavior. Clearly, such defiant and aggressive behavior patterns are more likely to appear in boys. Furthermore, Abikoff et al. (in press) and Schachar et al. (1986) have documented, as discussed in Chapter 2, that the presence of oppositional and aggressive behaviors produces a bias in teachers to infer the presence of attention problems and hyperactivity as well, even if the latter symptom patterns are not actually present. Thus, teachers may be prone to underdiagnose ADHD patterns in females. On the basis of data suggesting that girls with attention problems show significant impairment, both behaviorally and academically, and in order to prevent the underrecognition of females, McGee and Feehan (1991) recommend the use of same-gender norms to ascertain clinical levels of ADHD. This stance underscores the importance of obtaining rigorous and valid data with regard to symptom expression, patterns of impairment, etiologic factors, and treatment response in girls with ADHD.

SUMMARY

Perhaps the most salient theme of this entire book is the fundamental heterogeneity of attention deficits and hyperactivity in childhood. In this chapter I have reviewed several fundamental distinctions that have been applied to youngsters with ADHD over the years, emphasizing pervasive versus situational hyperactivity, attention deficit disorder with and without hyperactivity, and comorbidities with disruptive behavior disorders, learning disabilities, and internalizing disorders. In some of these domains rather substantial evidence exists with regard to qualitative differences between the subgroups under consideration: for example, ADD/WO appears to differ in fundamental ways from ADD/H. In other cases, it appears that subgroups are clearly different in a quantitative sense—for instance, ADHD youngsters with comorbid CD are at substantially higher risk for a number of concurrent and subsequent difficulties—with the possibility of qualitative distinctiveness not ruled out (e.g., Szatmari, Boyle, & Offord, 1989). For other areas, differences exist between subgroups but there is no indication to date of any fundamental, qualitative distinction. For instance, jointly ADHD and learning-disabled children clearly carry two sets of problematic functioning, yet these problem domains may be additive rather than indicative of a truly distinct subgroup.

Whether or not subgroups are qualitatively separable, evaluators and assessors need to pay far more attention to subgroups and comorbidity than has often been done in the past. Without assessments that can yield information on additional features or possible subtypes, we may misattribute risk factors, underlying etiologic mechanisms, follow-up status, or treatment response patterns to ADHD, when these features more accurately pertain to other dimensions or disorders. As argued by Caron and Rutter (1991), appropriate attention to true patterns of comorbidity in child psychopathology is quite likely to yield important insights regarding conceptual underpinnings and theoretical mechanisms. In short, the notion of a uniform disorder of ADHD flies in the face of both scientific progress and treatment efforts; only future research will reveal whether various subgroups or comorbid patterns signify true discontinuities in the externalizing, disinhibitory psychopathology of youngsters with attention deficits and hyperactivity.

NOTES

1. As noted in Chapter 1, the term *hyperkinesis* in ICD-9 refers to a narrower conception of attention deficits and hyperactivity than does the American view of ADHD, involving particularly severe levels of motoric dysregulation often accompanied by cognitive deficits. This definition of hyperkinesis requires the pervasive presence of symptomatology—in the home, school, and clinic. Yet even without resorting to the more restrictive definition of hyperkinesis, one can discuss the pervasive versus situational nature of ADHD, with the pervasive type referring to the presence of above-threshold symptomatology in multiple settings.

2. Note that whereas problems in both settings are required, information detailing such multisetting difficulties need only be reported by one source. Thus the *DSM-IV* criteria do not require that teachers as well as parents provide above-threshold symptom reports, only that at least one source presents information about problems in more than one setting.

3. Although the *DSM-IV* features an inattentive subtype of ADHD, marked by high symptom levels of inattention-disorganization symptoms but subthreshold indication of impulsivity-hyperactivity, this subgroup may differ from the ADD/WO categories featured in previous and contemporaneous research. Many of the latter samples have been defined on the basis of a different type of inattentiveness, denoted by daydreaming, sluggishness, and lack of motivation (as discussed below). I will therefore use the term *ADD/WO* rather than referring to the *DSM-IV* inattentive subtype in the ensuing discussion.

4. The proposed *DSM-IV* subcategory of an exclusively impulsive-hyperactive group of youngsters is controversial. As noted earlier, a small group of this type emerged in the field trials for *DSM-IV*, but half of these children were in the preschool age range. Presumably, their below-threshold scores on dimensions of inattention and disorganization reflected a lack of exposure to classroom activities that elicit such deficits. In defending the retention of this subcategory, Lahey (1993) has argued that their exclusion would prevent the opportunity for early intervention (see Campbell, 1990, for thorough explication of the issues surrounding preschool-aged children with ADHD).

5. The issue of comorbidity is receiving increasing clinical and theoretical attention in child psychopathology. Caron and Rutter (1991) provide a superb conceptual accounting of this construct. Among the highlights of their review is the demarcation of actual comorbidity—the concurrent presence of two or more distinct disorders—from artifactual comorbidity, which may include the diagnosing of two apparently distinct disorders that are actually different developmental manifestations of the same underlying process or that reflect imprecise definitions of pertinent categories. Indeed, the field requires greater understanding of key issues related to progressions and trajectories before comorbidity can be completely understood (Hinshaw et al., 1993).

6. Faraone et al. (1991b) concluded that the evidence could also favor a continuum of severity among the disruptive behavior disorders, with comorbid ADHD plus CD a more extreme variant of ADHD alone. The complicated patterns of cosegregation (i.e., joint

transmission) of the disorders within families were, in fact, compatible with either the "distinct subgroup" or the "continuum of severity" interpretations.

7. Such would be the expected outcome if the genetic predisposition to ADHD were polygenic (Cloninger et al., 1978).

5

COURSE, DEVELOPMENTAL PROGRESSIONS, AND PREDICTORS OF OUTCOME

What becomes of children with clinically significant levels of attention deficits and hyperactivity? As noted in Chapter 1, the prevailing view in past years was that this disorder held a good prognosis; indeed, the onset of puberty and adolescence supposedly witnessed remission of the symptom patterns. Today, however, results from several well-conducted prospective investigations have painted a far more sobering portrait of the natural history of ADHD. The goals for the current chapter are (a) to examine in more detail the types of long-term outcome that have been observed; (b) to discuss pertinent literature from the domain of developmental psychopathology, with the goal of providing theoretical underpinnings for understanding progressions; and (c) to scrutinize the developmental trajectories of youngsters with ADHD, in order to ascertain those variables or mechanisms in childhood that serve to predict long-term course. Featured will be discussion of the relative abilities of attention deficits/hyperactivity versus conduct problems/aggression in childhood to predict subsequent maladjustment. I also highlight, in passing, information regarding the critical issue of the predictability of ADHD in childhood from important variables in the preschool years (for a lucid overview of such issues, see Campbell, 1990).

NATURAL HISTORY OF ADHD

In most of the extant prospective follow-up investigations of children with ADHD into late adolescence or adulthood, diagnoses were made sufficiently long ago that current diagnostic standards did not apply and comorbidity of ADHD with other diagnostic categories was seldom specified. Because a key theme of this book has been that thorough assessment procedures and ample consideration of subgroups and comorbidity are of crucial importance regarding the types of inferences that can be made about ADHD youngsters (see Chapters 2 and 4), particular attention must be paid to sampling issues in discussions of follow-up reports.

Adolescent Outcome

Many early investigations of the long-term sequelae of childhood attention deficits and hyperactivity were retrospective or follow-back in nature, but such designs have clear limitations for making inferences regarding risk factors (Thorley, 1984). Klein and Mannuzza (1991) have recently reviewed, in concise fashion, the major prospective investigations of youngsters with childhood patterns of ADHD or hyperactivity; because of the superiority of prospective designs for making inferences about important predictive factors, I focus on these reports. Regarding outcome in adolescence, it is first clear that childhood symptom patterns tend to persist in a majority of individuals, with over two thirds of diagnosed children continuing to meet diagnostic criteria in mid- to late adolescence (e.g., Barkley, Fischer, Edelbrock, & Smallish, 1990; Gittelman et al., 1985; Mannuzza, Klein, Bonagura, et al., 1991). Second, antisocial behavior and substance abuse develop in one fourth to one half of the subjects followed into their teenage years, with delinquency or incarceration a common outcome (e.g., Gittelman et al., 1985; Loney, Whaley-Klahn, Kosier, & Conboy, 1983; Satterfield et al., 1982). In this regard, the careful follow-up reports of Gittelman et al. (1985) and Mannuzza, Klein, Bonagura, et al. (1991) are heuristic in that they reveal that the risk for adolescent substance abuse in youngsters with ADHD is mediated almost entirely by the development of antisocial behavior patterns. That is, unless antisocial behavior develops during adolescence, the risk of a substance use disorder is almost nonexistent. Also, regarding the high rates of delinquency found by Satterfield et al. (1982)—from 36% to 58% in various socioeconomic groups—it is unclear what proportion of the hyperactive youngsters during initial evaluations had comorbid aggressive-spectrum disorders. Indeed, discussion of the role of ADHD-related symptomatology versus aggression/conduct problems in predicting course is a central theme of this chapter.

Third, various indices of underachievement, cognitive dysfunction, and school failure are widespread in adolescents with histories of hyperactivity or ADHD (e.g., Fischer, Barkley, Edelbrock, & Smallish, 1990). Continuing behavioral symptomatology clearly compromises academic performance during adolescent years. Fourth, families of ADHD adolescents are more unstable and disharmonious than those of comparison youth, with a greater likelihood of separation or divorce (Barkley, Fischer, Edelbrock, & Smallish, 1990). Fifth, a sizable minority of youngsters with ADHD—perhaps a third—display remission of symptomatology by late adolescence, signifying that the disorder is heterogeneous not only symptomatically but also prognostically. Given the wide range of outcomes for children with clinically significant attention deficits and hyperactivity during preadolescence, I consider predictors of outcome status subsequently.

The investigations discussed above contain male probands almost exclusively. Mannuzza and Gittelman (1984) examined a small number of girls with clinical hyperactivity and found that rates of persistence of ADHD and of risk for antisocial behavior into adolescence were comparable to those for boys. Such preliminary findings bear replication.

Young Adult Outcome

Only a handful of prospective investigations have followed ADHD youngsters through young adulthood. The major findings are that despite overall improvement in functioning as subjects move into their 20s and early 30s, the risk for continuing problems with ADHD-related deficits, antisocial behavior, and in some cases substance abuse is substantially greater than in comparison groups. Note that these externalizing-spectrum disorders tend to cluster in certain individuals with ADHD histories: Childhood ADHD precipitates comorbid disruptive behavior disorders and substance abuse in certain cases, suggesting a subgroup that progresses from early ADHD through a chronic course of antisocial-spectrum disorders (Moffitt, in press). Police contacts are also higher in the adults with histories of ADHD than in control subjects, but as with substance abuse patterns, risk for such criminality appears to be elevated only if clearly antisocial behavior patterns develop over and above the persistence of ADHD (Klein & Mannuzza, 1991). In other words, continuing patterns of ADHD that are unaccompanied by the development of antisocial functioning appear not to predict increased risk for criminal activity.

Loney et al. (1983) and Mannuzza, Klein, and Addalli (1991) compared the long-term outcomes of boys with ADHD to those for their brothers. In both cases, although some comparisons were not significant, the boys with ADHD presented more severe antisocial outcomes in young adulthood, as indicated by a higher proportion of multiple diagnoses (Mannuzza, Klein, & Addalli, 1991) or by higher rates of incarceration (Loney et al., 1983). Thus, the negative course for ADHD cannot be explained completely by such shared factors between siblings as parental psychopathology or socioeconomic status.

It is worth reiterating (see Chapter 4) that the reports of Gittelman et al. (1985) and Mannuzza, Klein, Bonagura, et al. (1991) have failed to find any elevated risk for anxiety or mood disorders in their adolescent and adult probands, directly contradicting the contentions of Biederman and colleagues (e.g., Biederman, Munir, Knee, Armentano, et al., 1987) that ADHD and such internalizing disorders share common risks. Resolution of the widely disparate evidence regarding linkages between hyperactivity and internalizing conditions—in particular, mood disorders—is an important goal for future research.

In their long-term prospective study into adulthood performed in Montreal, Weiss and Hechtman (1986) have tended to find somewhat lower risks for antisocial behavior and criminality than American investigators, even though risks are still elevated above those of comparison subjects. Furthermore, a small subgroup of their adult sample appears to evidence severe maladjustment and even suicidal ideation and attempts.[1] Whether differences in results across longitudinal studies are attributable to divergent sampling methods, possible cohort effects, the role of different cultures, or other artifacts is presently indeterminate.

Overall, ADHD is far from a benign disorder: It carries significant risk for antisocial outcomes and for continuing patterns of disinhibited behavior, cognitive dysfunction, and interpersonal difficulties. The clear majority of ADHD youngsters maintain full symptom patterns through mid-adolescence, with a substantial plurality persisting into young adulthood. Significant antisocial behavior plagues one fourth to one third or more of this population; indeed, a sizable subgroup is at risk for multiple disorders, including substance abuse, during late adolescent development. Yet symptomatic remission and even positive outcomes await a significant minority of ADHD youngsters as they mature. The key issues that remain involve understanding developmental pathways and elucidating key variables and processes that mediate outcome.

DEVELOPMENTAL PROGRESSIONS
AND PREDICTORS OF OUTCOME

Conceptual Issues

Determining the causal processes leading to follow-up status is fraught with difficulty. For example, consider two hypothetical groups of youngsters of the same social class, gender, ethnic background, and family composition who display equivalent levels of attention deficits and disinhibition at age 8. If such groups, 10 years later, diverge with respect such important variables as completion of school, maintenance of ADHD-related symptomatology, social adjustment, or antisocial behavior, a logical goal would be to attempt to determine the preexisting variables separating the children at the initial assessment point. Assume that the first group, which displays the worse outcome picture, had been markedly more aggressive than the second at 8 years of age. The explanation could readily be proposed that their more negative outcome represented the persistence of the trait of aggression/antisociability.

Yet many problems with such specification of predictive factors immediately ensue. A plausible rival explanation for this "persistent trait" model is that the former group has continued to experience a more discordant family environment across the 10-year time period (e.g., Barkley, Fischer, Edelbrock, & Smallish, 1990). If this were the case, the proximal causes of both the early aggression and the later maladjustment/antisocial features could well be environmental in nature (see Lewis, 1990, for further consideration of such issues). Looking even further back in time, however, may reveal that prior causal factors—such as antisocial functioning in one or both parents—comprise "third variables" driving (a) the early disinhibition of the child, (b) the family disharmony displayed at initial and follow-up assessments, and (c) the adolescent display of antisocial behavior.[2] In this scenario the familial "causation" may involve heritable factors as well as gene-environment correlations that unfold with development. In short, it should be apparent that the search for predictive factors, like the exploration of etiologic agents (see Chapter 3), is fraught with interpretive difficulty.

Before examining available evidence regarding the predictability of the natural history of ADHD in more depth, a brief glance at several key issues from the field of developmental psychopathology may be helpful (see Campbell, 1990, Lewis, 1990, and Rutter, 1989, for elaboration of these theoretical concerns). First, a major debate in developmental psychology and developmental psychopathology relates to the continuity versus discontinuity of cognitive functioning, behavior patterns, and emotional development across the life span. The predominant view until recently has been that (a) early manifestations of externalizing behavior in the preschool years are transitory phenomena and that (b) ADHD-related symptomatology remits by adolescence (for reviews, see Barkley, 1990; Campbell, 1990). Thus, discontinuity was the prevailing view. Yet empirical evidence within the past 15 years supports considerable continuity from preschool to middle childhood with respect to acting-out and disinhibited behavior (Campbell, 1990; Richman et al., 1982).[3] Furthermore, the above discussion on natural history yielded persuasive evidence with regard to the continuity of problem behavior for a majority of ADHD children through mid-adolescence. Thus, continuity in the domains under consideration is apparent for many children.

By adulthood, however, general improvements in core problem domains restrict such continuity to a smaller subgroup. Furthermore, at the earliest stages of development, only limited evidence exists for the continuity of difficult temperament patterns during infancy into disinhibited behavior in subsequent years (Maziade, Cote, Bernier, Boutin, & Thivierge, 1989). Thus, substantial discontinuity may pertain to these particular developmental transitions. Yet before continuity is ruled out altogether, recall the discussion in Chapter 1 of heterotypic continuity: For some individuals there may be strong consistency in developmental course, but the persisting trait may change form across time. In other words, perhaps the developmental changes across major life periods (e.g., from infancy to childhood or from adolescence to adulthood) are sufficiently salient that we should refocus our discussion on the predictability or coherence of behavior rather than its strict continuity (Sroufe, 1979). It may be possible to understand developmental change as following lawfully from key biological, psychological, and/or familial processes even though overt behavior patterns do not maintain consistent expression. Finally, a host of factors may act in concert to yield predictable or continuous development. As discussed in Chapter 4, biological and environmental interactions and transactional paths appear to be the rule for the unfolding of ADHD.

With respect to the predictability of the course of ADHD, a second overarching issue relates to the types of pathways and trajectories that characterize development. For some processes, predictive paths may be direct, in that a variable at initial assessment exerts an independent influence on the outcome domain. Yet many causal processes may be indirect, in that the primary influence of certain predictors is on mediating variables, which in turn influence the outcome of interest. As just one example, when Paternite and Loney (1980) examined the effects of social class and family climate on the aggressive behavior that often accompanies ADHD, the effects of SES were indirect: They were mediated by their influence on family disharmony, which directly related to aggressive behavior.

Another perspective on developmental persistence and causation comes from Caspi and Moffitt (in press), who distinguish cumulative from interactional continuity of behavior. In cumulative continuity, the effects of a variable of interest are not only indirect but cascading: A sequence of events triggered by the variable leads to the outcome of interest. Thus, as a hypothetical example regarding the predictability of later aggression from early inattention, attentional deficits in early childhood may trigger poor development of reading readiness skills, leading to frustration that fuels underachievement and acting-out behavior. No direct link between the early attention problems and the eventual school failure and antisociability would exist in this scenario; instead, the progression is cumulative. Interactional continuity, on the other hand, refers to the kinds of patterns in which certain behavioral tendencies generate social interactions that promote emotional or behavioral outcomes in the immediate interaction. For example, high rates of negative behavior (tantrums, irritability) may elicit ineffective caretaking, which itself promotes high rates of aggression.

Such processes and terms are not mutually exclusive. Certain causal agents or predictors may exert effects that are both direct and indirect, cumulative and interactional. Early deficits in receptive and particularly in expressive language abilities have been implicated as a risk factor for subsequent ADHD (see Chapter 3). Such delays may operate distally and indirectly by shaping the child's eventual school failure, which may in turn lead to eventual exacerbation of attention problems and disinhibition. Such effects are cumulative, but language deficits may also exert more immediate interactional effects via parental frustration at communicating with an unresponsive child. Several different causal chains involving the same underlying variables may therefore operate simultaneously.

For another example with pertinence to ADHD, Moffitt (1993) has noted that although neuropsychological deficits are associated with the display of aggressive conduct problems, the norm is for such neuropsychological processing deficits to improve with time. How, then, are we to explain the escalating problems that characterize many youngsters with aggressive conduct disorder (which, as discussed in Chapter 4, is clearly linked with ADHD)? Moffitt (1993) believes that the causal effects of neuropsychological processing difficulties are distal and cumulative rather than direct. That is, these cognitive problems trigger school failure and demoralization—as well as poor parent-child bonding in the earliest years—which propel the child toward antisocial behavior in cumulative fashion, even though the neuropsychological processes themselves may be improving and are probably not immediate causes of aggressive actions. The overarching point is that causal processes are complex and interactive rather than easily specified and static.

The Roles of Aggression and ADHD Symptomatology as Predictors of Subsequent Antisocial Behavior

Although ADHD youngsters are at risk for a host of negative outcomes, particular attention has been directed to their propensity for antisocial behavior and related substance abuse, in part because of the clear impairment engendered by such sequelae. In a synthetic review article, Lilienfeld and Waldman (1990) critically examined existing evidence regarding the predictability of adult antisocial behavior patterns from childhood attention deficits and hyperactivity. Their conclusion was that, given the marked overlap in childhood between aggressive behavior patterns and ADHD per se (Hinshaw, 1987b), investigators must make a systematic attempt to tease apart such behavior patterns in predictive reports. Otherwise, sequelae of the childhood aggression and conduct disorder will mistakenly be attributed to the ADHD symptomatology. In the case of family history, for example—as discussed in Chapters 1 and 3—it is clear that the antisocial spectrum disorders once attributed to childhood hyperactivity are now known to pertain specifically to aggression and conduct disorder in youth (Lahey, Piacentini, et al., 1988; Schachar & Wachsmuth, 1990).

In seminal research efforts for the field, Loney and colleagues have performed longitudinal research directly testing the predictive efficacy of childhood dimensions of "aggression" (combining features of overt acting out, covert antisocial behavior, and negative affect) versus "hyperactivity" (a composite of the core features of today's conception of ADHD) in predicting adolescent outcome in a sample of children with the former diagnosis of minimal brain dysfunction (Loney et al., 1981; see also Loney et al., 1983). Importantly, whereas the hyperactivity dimension independently predicted adolescent achievement in school, it did not yield independent predictions of any behavior patterns. Aggression, in fact, was the specific predictor of antisocial behavior, drug use patterns, and even hyperactivity itself at follow-up. Milich and Loney (1979) interpreted such findings in light of evidence that aggressive behavior patterns are shaped in large part by discordant and coercive parent-child interchange (Patterson, 1982), which may serve as the key determinants of prognosis. In recent follow-up analyses (Kramer, 1993; Roberts, 1993), it was determined that such differential predictability was maintained at follow-up into adulthood, with hyperactivity specifically predicting alcohol use but aggression independently presaging antisocial behavior and substance use disorders other than alcoholism.

Given the strong evidence for (a) the persisting nature of aggression and antisocial behavior throughout childhood and adolescence (Loeber, 1982) and (b) the linkages between ADHD and significant levels of aggression (Hinshaw, 1987b), only research designs that specifically yield separable dimensions or subgroups at initial assessment periods can hope to disentangle the nature of predictive relationships. On the basis of the findings of Loney and colleagues, as well as reappraisals of other outcomes in the field, many commentators today assign the greatest weight to childhood aggression regarding prediction of subsequent outcome (see Lilienfeld & Waldman, 1990). It must be remembered, in considering such a viewpoint, that measures of child aggression may serve as representations of a large number of child, family, and neighborhood variables; aggressive behavior may be a proxy for such diverse processes as parental psychopathology, discordant and abusive parental practices, impoverished neighborhoods, or other predisposing factors (Barkley, 1990; Milich & Loney, 1979). Thus, as I have emphasized throughout, predictive paths are likely to be multifactorial (see also Ohman & Magnusson, 1987).

Despite evidence for the predictability of key outcomes from early aggression, scrutiny of additional reports suggests strongly that dimensions of inattention and impulsivity-hyperactivity may themselves have major roles in propelling a negative course. I now present more detailed consideration of this line of evidence. First, in an examination of predictors of antisocial behavior in the Cambridge Study for Delinquent Development that has been conducted in London, Farrington, Loeber, and Van Kammen (1990) discovered that a behavioral cluster they termed *hyperactive-impulsive-attention problem* (HIA), assessed at 8 to 10 years of age, predicted self-reported and official criminality in adolescence and young adulthood independently of child aggression. For most outcomes, the effects of HIA behaviors and aggression were additive. Crucially, for the important outcome of chronic offending by age 25 (denoted by six or more offenses), the prediction from early HIA was nearly as strong as that from early aggression, and no interactive effects were yielded. Thus, independent effects of ADHD-spectrum behaviors to important antisocial outcomes were discerned.

Similarly, albeit with a different age range and different operationalization of key variables, Magnusson (1987) discovered that a teacher-rated index of early-adolescent "motor restlessness" exerted stronger associations with criminality 15 years later than did teacher-appraised "aggression," with effects of the joint predictors additive in nature. Such single-item predictors cannot be mistaken, however, for syndromal ADHD or conduct disorder.

In an elegant investigation that also made use of dimensional predictors, Moffitt (1990) studied the predictability of early- and mid-adolescent antisocial behavior from preschool and grade-school indices of aggression and attention deficits/hyperactivity. Briefly, even with statistical control of age-5 aggression, early elementary ADHD symptomatology predicted the adolescent outcomes. Furthermore, indicating the complexity and interactive nature of causal pathways, the early attention problems/hyperactivity revealed statistical interactions with both low verbal IQ and family adversity in predicting adolescent antisocial behavior. In other words, the effects of ADHD symptoms on adolescent antisocial behavior were qualified by intraindividual and environmental variables, such that low IQ and significant family adversity enhanced the risk posed by the inattentive, impulsive, and hyperactive behavioral problems. Neuropsychological deficits in childhood may also enter into the predictive equation (Moffitt & Silva, 1988), such that the overlap of early attention deficits/hyperactivity with neuropsychological processing difficulties are highly related to the persistence of antisocial behavior patterns.

In short, despite the known persistence of the trait of aggression/antisocial behavior, dimensions of inattention and disinhibition in childhood produce independent risk for adolescent antisociability. Furthermore, ADHD-related behaviors appear to interact dynamically with cognitive and family-level processes to exacerbate the risk for the maintenance or intensification of severe externalizing behavior.

The investigations under discussion employed dimensional scores of inattentive/hyperactive behaviors as predictor measures. Even though such dimensions predicted subsequent antisocial behavior independently of dimensions of early aggressive behavior, it would also be helpful to compare the longitudinal course of subgroups of ADHD youngsters derived on the basis of presence or absence of significant levels of childhood aggression. Pertinent investigations must contend with an important conceptual and methodologic issue, namely the developmental sensitivity of the measures of child externalizing behavior. For example, in the above-cited report of Mannuzza, Klein, Bonagura, et al. (1991), the authors contended that ADHD in the absence of aggressive conduct problems predicts later antisociability, in that only one child in the sample (which had a mean age of 7.3 years) had been diagnosed with conduct disorder (CD) during childhood. Yet the severity of the constituent behaviors involved in the criteria for CD make it extremely difficult for a young child to qualify for such a diagnosis; utilizing this category as the index of early aggression may well miss the presence of more developmentally relevant indicators. Loeber, Lahey, and Thomas (1991) argue that oppositional-defiant disorder (ODD), which entails high levels of defiance, anger, and irritability, is such a precursor to later CD in many youth. Although the validity of ODD is hotly debated, the pertinent point is that indicators of the construct of aggression and conduct problems must be developmentally attuned in order to ascertain their independence from or linkages with ADHD symptomatology regarding the ability to predict important long-term outcomes.

A Subgroup With Early Onset

Resolution of the findings from the above-cited investigations is problematic. On the one hand, early aggression appears to be quite stable; its comorbidity with ADHD may explain the development of antisocial behavior in selected youngsters. Yet the independent predictability of delinquent and antisocial outcomes from early ADHD-spectrum behaviors has also been established. How can such results be rectified?

Our research strategies in the field are typically variable centered, meaning that we examine dimensions of behavior for consistency over time or for their ability to predict other outcomes. Yet by failing to pay appropriate attention to (a) developmental processes and (b) the existence of discrete subgroups, our focus on dimensions and/or variables may miss the operation of different developmental trajectories in important subpopulations. This line of reasoning has recently been applied to delinquent and antisocial behavior by Moffitt (in press), who has discerned two fundamentally divergent categories of delinquent adolescents. By far the most common group (termed "adolescence-limited") displays noteworthy criminal activity that arises for the first time in early to mid-adolescence, featuring a preponderance of nonaggressive (covert) actions that typically desist by late adolescence. Importantly, girls and boys display nearly equal rates of such adolescence-limited delinquency, which is not associated with preexisting cognitive or behavioral deficits.

On the other hand, a much smaller group of "life-course-persistent" antisocial youth are overwhelmingly male and display overt aggression in adolescence. Such youth typically display markedly defiant and aggressive behavior from an early age; an alternate name for this group could be "early onset" (Hinshaw et al., 1993). Critically, the histories of such adolescents are also marked by (a) cognitive/neuropsychological dysfunction, particularly in the verbal sphere; (b) extreme family disharmony; and (c) attention deficits/hyperactivity.

From a cross-sectional perspective, the covert antisocial actions of adolescence-limited youth appear similar to those of the life-course-persistent group, in that severity levels are comparable. Thus, unless the subgroups are discerned on the basis of age of onset and key developmental features—particularly, histories of attention deficits and hyperactivity—essential information will be lost by lumping together all antisocial behavior (Moffitt, in press). Childhood diagnostic categories must therefore begin to incorporate developmental features rather than reflecting static entities at a purely descriptive level (see Hinshaw et al., 1993).

The clear role of early attention problems and disinhibition in the genesis of the life-course-persistent group is pertinent to the ongoing discussion regarding the predictive validity of ADHD symptomatology. For children diagnosed with ADHD, the concurrent presence of verbal deficits, neuropsychological dysfunction, and poor family management practices may combine to promote an increasingly antisocial trajectory. As noted earlier, it is the interaction and active transaction among such risk factors that appears to predict the later expression of severely antisocial functioning (Hinshaw, in press). Investigators of ADHD and of developmental psychopathology in general must incorporate processes as diverse as neuropsychology, family relations, school climate, peer relations, and behavioral disinhibition to fully explore developmental progressions.

ADHD and Underachievement in Predicting Long-Term Outcome

Academic failure clearly incurs major consequences in our achieve- ment-oriented society.[4] For many years investigators have noted an association between academic underachievement and externalizing behavior in childhood and adolescence, with the predominant theories implicating (a) poor achievement as a cause or predictor of later aggression or (b) early aggressive behavior as causal of subsequent school failure. In a recent review of the evidence regarding such unidirectional hypotheses (Hinshaw, 1992b), I emphasized that attention deficits and hyperactivity are directly implicated in such causal chains. In the following summation of the evidence for developmental progressions involving ADHD and underachievement, I emphasize the central role of attention problems and disinhibition in mediating long-term outcome and the complexity of developmental pathways in the field.

First, scrutiny of available data regarding linkages between underachievement and externalizing behavior reveals that the specific association, in childhood, pertains to attention deficits/hyperactivity rather than aggression or conduct disorder, again highlighting the importance of separating these subdomains of externalizing behavior. An exemplary study in this regard was performed by Frick et al. (1991), who found that the apparent covariation between CD and underachievement in a clinic sample was entirely accounted for by the association between CD and ADHD; only the latter showed an independent association with learning disabilities. By adolescence, however, a considerable data base supports the linkage between antisocial behavior and delinquency, on the one hand, and a variety of indices of underachievement and school failure, on the other. Attention deficits and hyperactivity may therefore be implicated in the progression to the adolescent association between acting-out behavior and academic deficiencies.

How do ADHD-related symptoms play a role in the subsequent link between antisocial activity and school failure? Several themes emerge from analysis of prospective investigations. First, overarching theories attempting to account for the interrelationships among ADHD, underachievement, and later antisocial actions across all children are likely to be misguided. Specifically, the global unidirectional models (i.e., early underachievement predicts later externalizing behavior; early display of disruptive behavior interferes with learning) have received sparse empirical support. Although it is often the case that cognitive and learning problems in elementary school predict subsequent acting-out behavior, this relationship typically disappears once the early link between learning problems and attention deficits/hyperactivity is controlled. In other words, the confounded nature of the domains of interest during preliminary assessment periods clouds the longitudinal predictability of one domain from the other.

Furthermore, early signs of externalizing behavior and cognitive readiness problems appear to be associated during preschool years. The presence of such a relationship before the start of formal schooling suggests strongly that one or more "third variables" underlie the overlap between achievement and externalizing behavior that unfolds with development. One potential candidate involves early deficits in language, which appear to predict both subsequent ADHD and learning problems (Hinshaw, 1992b). Even further back in the causal chain, neurodevelopmental delays could predict, in certain subgroups, both delayed language and the eventual presence of both behavioral disinhibition and underachievement. In addition, as explicated by Richman et al. (1982), family dysfunction appears to interact with early language difficulties in shaping risk for behavioral and learning problems. In short, causal pathways related to ADHD and its natural history are not likely to be direct or univariate.

Distinct types of developmental progression from underachievement and externalizing behavior to more frank antisocial outcomes are likely to characterize different subgroups of youngsters. In other words, the field may be misled by seeking grand predictive models when qualitatively different processes operate for different subtypes. For example, Maughan, Gray, and Rutter (1985) discovered that, among a group of learning-disabled 10-year-olds with no signs of contemporaneous aggression or antisocial behavior, a minority developed antisocial behavior patterns by follow-up in adolescence. For this group, at least, the frustrations accruing to deficient school performance may have fueled resentment and demoralization, which, in turn, propelled exposure to deviant peer groups and antisocial activities. For other subgroups, however, comorbidity between adolescent underachievement and acting-out behavior may stem from a history of ADHD and neuropsychological difficulties (Moffitt & Silva, 1988). To reiterate a common theme of this book, different developmental trajectories appear to characterize diverging subgroups. The chief assertion of this section is that attentional deficits and hyperactivity are closely tied to cognitive problems, learning deficiencies, and underachievement; such links are likely to fuel the further development of antisocial behavior in a number of children.

WHICH FACTORS RELIABLY PREDICT LONG-TERM OUTCOME IN CHILDREN WITH ADHD?

The previous discussion has probed the complex relationships that pertain to the role of early attention deficits/hyperactivity in shaping antisocial behavior and underachievement. Within samples of ADHD youngsters per se, a simpler question involves ascertaining the factors that appear to predict either deficient or positive long-term outcome. Despite several attempts to yield answers, clear solutions have evaded investigators.

Several methodologic issues pertain to understanding such predictive relationships. First, with a large number of potential antecedent variables (compounded by a relative paucity of available subjects in prospective investigations), maintaining acceptable levels of statistical rigor is problematic. Second, models that can account for interactions among predictor variables—potentially elucidating critical causal mechanisms that join intraindividual, familial, and systems factors—are rare in the field (for an exception, see Moffitt, 1990). Third, because empirical predictions capitalize on chance associations in a given data set, any predictive relationships that are found require cross-validation, ideally in a new sample.

Regarding specific data, the prospective reports of Loney et al. (1983), Weiss and Hechtman (1986), and Mannuzza, Gittelman, Konig, and Giampino (1990) all yielded several predictive relationships between early-assessed variables and later outcomes in their samples of youngsters with ADHD (or earlier diagnostic categories corresponding to ADHD). Univariate relations found by Loney et al. (1983) between family size and IQ, and between family size and antisocial behavior, have not, however, been replicated. Furthermore, the significant associations between some of the predictors and outcomes in Weiss and Hechtman (1986) emerged from a large number of univariate correlations; cross-validation is essential. Indeed, without cross-validation strategies, any relationships that emerge between baseline and outcome variables may be spurious, capitalizing on chance relationships within the sample.

Mannuzza et al. (1990) made an explicit attempt to cross-validate their predictions of adolescent outcome in ADHD youngsters via statistical jackknife procedures. (These techniques simulate the presence of an independent sample for validation.) The results of this laudable effort, however, revealed that none of the initial predictors held up when the statistical validation procedure was applied. In other words, although statistically significant, the predictive relationships were sufficiently tenuous that they did not replicate. Given the wide variability in the adolescent and adult outcomes of youngsters with ADHD, robust predictions would be of extreme value both theoretically and clinically; the field awaits sufficient sample sizes and sufficiently astute methodologies to ascertain replicable predictions.

SUMMARY

The natural history of ADHD is plagued by risk for continuing symptomatology related to attention deficits and hyperactivity as well as for cognitive deficits, antisocial behavior, and in some cases substance abuse. Yet a sizable number of ADHD youth go on to develop positive outcomes; variability at follow-up status is quite large. Although aggression in childhood may be a more specific predictor of later antisociability and substance abuse than is ADHD-related symptomatology per se, attention deficits/hyperactivity independently predict key outcomes in a number of cases, with complex chains of disinhibitory behavior, adverse family circumstance, and diminished cognitive performance combining to enhance risk. Also, learning deficits are associated with ADHD in childhood, and this combination is particularly likely to presage the later link between delinquency/antisocial behavior and school failure in adolescence. Unfortunately, robust predictors of long-term follow-up status of ADHD children have evaded detection, particularly because of the failures to replicate promising variables when cross-validation is attempted. Overall, ascertaining processes specific to subgroups may be more pertinent to the goal of predicting and explaining status at follow-up than are overarching predictions across the entire range of youngsters with ADHD.

NOTES

1. Another provocative finding from their extensive longitudinal investigation is that the hyperactive youngsters tended to perform better once they left school and entered the job market. The interpretation is that the less rigorous structure of most jobs, in comparison with the roteness of secondary school, promotes lower rates of symptom expression. Such a perspective again reflects the importance of maintaining a social ecological perspective with regard to the expression of attention deficits and hyperactivity (Whalen & Henker, 1980).

2. Indeed, Lahey, Hartdagen, et al. (1988) showed that, in a clinic sample of boys with conduct disorder (CD), the effects of parental divorce on CD status were no longer significant once antisocial personality disorder in the fathers was controlled. Similarly, Frick et al. (1992) found a relationship between interview-disclosed patterns of poor family management styles and the CD status of the sons; but this effect dissipated when antisocial patterns in the fathers were statistically controlled. In short, the effects of parental antisociability are powerful predictors of aggression and CD in childhood, outweighing other important familial variables.

3. Campbell (1990) has summarized her extensive longitudinal research program on 3- and 4-year-olds who display significant levels of disinhibition and hyperactivity. Approximately half of these youngsters show continuity by age 9, in the form of the meeting of full clinical criteria for ADHD. The two strongest factors in predicting later ADHD from preschool-aged difficulties are (a) the severity of the initial presenting problems and (b) coercive mother-child interactional style during early assessments (see Campbell & Ewing, 1990). Richman et al. (1982) present another compelling case for continuity; their data reveal the interactive roles of family disharmony, cognitive and language delays, and neighborhood factors in maintaining the persistence of early problem behavior. Clearly, severe levels of ADHD-related problems in the preschool years are not transitory problems for many children.

4. Many concepts and terms can be invoked to describe school failure and academic underachievement. Some variables, like retention and placement in special education classes, appear to reflect problem behavior as much as they denote learning problems per se (Hinshaw, 1992b). Regarding mastery of academic material, low achievement in school—for whatever causes, including subaverage intellectual abilities—can be distinguished from what are termed specific learning disabilities, which involve deficiencies in academic performance that are not accounted for by lowered intelligence. The importance of distinguishing IQ-discrepant underachievement from globally low achievement has been debated for decades (Rutter & Yule, 1975); for theoretical and practical reasons, it is important to consider both types of learning inefficiency in relation to problem behavior.

6

INTERVENTION STRATEGIES

Intervention for children with attention deficits and hyperactivity encompasses polar opposites. For example, the field has witnessed, over the years, both excellent science and fervent political beliefs, with each vying for center stage in the public eye. In addition, treatment issues have engendered both consensus and controversy, as exemplified by the strong evidence for short-term benefits from major treatments as well as the contentious debates regarding pharmacologic interventions, in particular. Furthermore, both investigators and the public appear to vacillate between optimism and pessimism regarding the success of various intervention strategies. Charting a course through the disparate findings, conceptual problems, methodologic issues, and policy implications related to intervention for ADHD is a difficult task.

Several points of perspective may help to frame treatment-related issues. First, no other child disorder has had as much controlled research performed regarding treatment. Clear evidence exists for clinically significant short-term benefits from established interventions—stimulant medication and behavioral procedures—for a majority of youngsters with ADHD. Although these treatments exhibit marked effectiveness, the quality with which such strategies are implemented and evaluated in clinical practice is often inadequate, and success rates are not universal. Too often, in fact, treatment options appear to begin and end with single interventions delivered in isolation and without adequate monitoring of efficacy. Because combinations of efficacious treatments are receiving increased attention as the preferred intervention strategy for this disorder (Pelham & Hinshaw, 1992), I highlight here the practical, methodologic, and conceptual problems related to implementing and evaluating combined interventions.

Second, the use of medications to manage a behavioral disorder continues to generate heated debate. The often vehement opinions voiced in the media and by various advocacy groups have served to polarize opinion, sometimes precluding rational discourse about research agendas and policy implications. Most recently, the Church of Scientology-sponsored Citizen's Commission on Human Rights mounted a vociferous campaign in the late 1980s against stimulant medications, particularly methylphenidate (Ritalin) (see Barkley, 1990; Cowart, 1988). Furthermore because misinformation abounds about available types of intervention, families are prone to gravitate towards a host of nonvalidated treatments, which continue to proliferate for children with ADHD. Carefully designed treatment studies and wide dissemination of pertinent information to parents, educators, and primary care professionals appear to be the antidotes to unwarranted assertions and false claims.

Perhaps the key issue for the field is that despite clear short-term success for validated interventions, long-term efficacy remains elusive. Indeed, a marked disparity exists between the short-range effectiveness of both pharmacologic and behavioral treatments and their apparent lack of benefit for altering the course of the disorder. The persisting and often escalating difficulties displayed by ADHD children in domains that are predictive of long-range functioning demand the development of interventions that target such key areas as control of aggression, peer relationships, and academic achievement. Whether long-term intervention strategies directed toward such central areas of functioning can alter the course of the disorder is, at present, indeterminate.

The chief goals for this chapter are to highlight the benefits and drawbacks of interventions in current use and to discuss the knowledge gaps that prevent promotion of long-term change. To organize the voluminous information that the field has accumulated with respect to intervention, I first address, in concise fashion, underlying theoretical issues regarding choice of treatment strategies. I then consider, in turn, pharmacologic and behavioral treatments, focusing on both the domains in which benefits have been documented and areas of limitation for each modality. Space limitations permit only cursory coverage of alternative interventions (dietary, biofeedback, expressive therapy) that are frequently used. Finally, I move to consideration of treatment combinations, closing with discussion of current planning for a collaborative, multisite intervention trial sponsored by the National Institute of Mental Health, which aims to systematically evaluate intensive, long-term treatment treatments for ADHD children and their families.

CONCEPTUAL UNDERPINNINGS
OF TREATMENT

A crucial issue pertains to the theoretical basis for our choice of interventions. If the field could base its treatment procedures on validated conceptions regarding important mechanisms that underlie symptom display and functional impairment, intervention efforts would have a greater likelihood of effecting change that would generalize across settings and persist over time. Our interventions, in this scenario, would be curative or restorative rather than simply palliative or symptom focused. Yet given the lack of consensus as to the underlying nature of ADHD (see Chapter 3), it may come as no surprise that the field's current treatment strategies lack a coherent conceptual base.

It might be argued that this state of affairs is not as pessimistic as it may sound. Recall from Chapter 3 that effective treatment strategies need not be directed towards primary causes of a condition (if these are, indeed, even known). For example, as noted earlier, effective treatment of the genetic disorder PKU may be exclusively dietary; in addition, cognitive therapy for depression can be quite successful, even though maladaptive cognitions do not appear to be causal of depressive episodes. It may be possible, in terms of this line of thinking, to aim interventions directly at symptom patterns, with the hope of alleviating disruptive behavioral processes and of preventing further escalation into a more negative course.

At a minimum, however, it would be crucial to know which problem areas are most related to the development of continuing dysfunction, because these should become primary intervention targets. Thus investigators must be keenly aware of developmental progressions and must strive to direct treatments toward the problem domains that truly relate to poor prognosis. At a deeper level, treatment directed towards theoretically and empirically established underlying mechanisms, even if these are not primary causes, should yield gains that are more fundamental and persistent. In the area of interpersonal and peer difficulties, for example, a key question pertains to the presence of underlying skill deficits in children with ADHD. If children with attention problems and hyperactivity do not actually display deficits in the processing of social information or in basic social skills (see Chapter 3), then the types of intervention under the rubric of "social skills training" would appear to be misguided (see Hinshaw, 1992c; Whalen & Henker, 1992). Teaching already-learned skills might not address these children's well-established difficulties in skill *performance*, which may relate to motivational or self-regulatory processes; intervention should perhaps focus on altering social agendas and on concentrated rehearsal of skills under increasingly realistic situational parameters.

From a broader perspective, most of the treatments in existence for ADHD are evaluated in an acute fashion, over periods of weeks or months. The assumption is that such short-term "doses" of intervention should be able to alter functioning, even when the treatments are terminated. If, however, the accurate model of ADHD and of other externalizing disorders is one of chronic disabilities (Barkley, 1987; Kazdin, 1987), then the field should not expect any short-term, acute treatments, even those with impressive benefits, to yield long-term gains. No one would expect that several months of insulin treatment would be sufficient to eradicate diabetes. Our intervention strategies for ADHD require far longer time spans than are currently investigated or practiced.

Despite the potential for empirical justification of some components of treatment packages, the lack of a theoretical basis for current interventions is still a troubling issue (R. Barkley, personal communication, February, 1993). Although post hoc justifications for the major, validated treatments abound—for example, stimulants affect the key neurotransmitter systems implicated in the psychopathology of ADHD; behavioral interventions aim to modify the contingencies of a child with faulty responsivity to reward or to normalize coercive family functioning that may promote aggressive behavior—the field's lack of certainty regarding the nature of attention deficits and hyperactivity precludes any real theoretical justification for treatments in use. In addition, many treatment strategies that are widely used (e.g., dietary or allergy-related interventions) appear to be predicated on unwarranted theoretical notions (e.g., McGee et al., 1993). Whereas there may be small consolation in knowing that the same state of affairs—lack of theoretical basis for major treatments, faulty underlying assumptions for alternatives, lack of connection between short- and long-term outcomes—pertains to nearly every other child and adult behavioral or mental disorder currently under investigation, clearer understanding of the nature of attention deficits and hyperactivity should yield crucial perspectives on intervention that will guide our search for durable treatment strategies.[1]

PHARMACOLOGIC INTERVENTION FOR ADHD

Overview of Stimulant Medications

The use of stimulant medications to treat behavior disorders in children dates to the 1930s, when Bradley (1937) used Benzedrine for youngsters attending a residential treatment facility. The observations were that this stimulant enhanced the motivation and effort of the treated children, whose problems appear to have included a wide range of disorders including but not limited to what today would be termed ADHD. Even in this early research, important benefits on achievement and aggressive behavior were noted, although methodologic standards were not high (see Hinshaw, 1991, for a review). It was not until the 1950s and 1960s, when the stimulant methylphenidate (MPH) was synthesized and when narrower notions of hyperkinesis and hyperactivity were replacing theories of minimal brain dysfunction, that stimulants received both closer empirical scrutiny and wider clinical use.

Scores of controlled investigations in the past 30 years have documented the benefits of stimulant medications on the core symptomatology and related difficulties of ADHD. With these medications, most youngsters sustain attention better in class, comply more readily with teacher and parent requests, display better organization, show less impulsivity in behavioral response, and exhibit less motoric movement (for systematic reviews of the history and efficacy of stimulants, see Barkley, 1990; Gadow, 1992; Greenhill & Osman, 1991; and Ross & Ross, 1982, to name several).[2] Although MPH has received, by far, the most research attention, recent evidence strongly suggests that the benefits of dextroamphetamine (DEX) may have been overlooked, given suggestive evidence that a significant percentage of youngsters show a favorable response to this stimulant and not to MPH (Elia, Borcherding, Rapoport, & Keysor, 1991). Largely because of the predominantly positive findings regarding stimulant effects, and also because of aggressive marketing by manufacturers, stimulant treatment is relatively widespread in the United States, although wide temporal and geographic fluctuations in prevalence rates for stimulant prescriptions are known to occur.

Indeed the systematic data of Safer and Krager (1988) indicate that, in Baltimore County, Maryland, nearly 90% of youngsters diagnosed with ADHD have received stimulants at some point during childhood, comprising over 6% of the school-aged population. In some locales, overly inclusive diagnostic criteria and poor assessment practices, as well as overzealous physicians or schools, can lead to inappropriately high utilization rates. The more restrictive diagnostic criteria in *DSM-IV*, stipulating significant levels of long-standing attention problems and/or disinhibition both at home and school, may facilitate appropriate caution in making a diagnosis and in prescribing pharmacologic intervention. Furthermore, because the use of medications to engender behavioral compliance may be particularly inappropriate unless benefits in key domains of developmental significance (e.g., control of aggression, peer relationships, and academic performance) are also facilitated, I pay particular attention to medication effects on such domains.

In attempting to provide a concise yet coherent perspective on key issues surrounding stimulant intervention, I address, in the following sections, (a) facts about the time course of stimulant treatment, (b) short- and long-term effects of these medications, (c) side effects, and (d) alternative pharmacologic agents. My aim is to document the clear benefits as well as potential limitations of medication interventions while setting the stage for consideration of alternative and adjunctive interventions.

Time-Course of Stimulant Actions

Although they may seem of peripheral importance, the time-response properties of stimulant medications have intriguing parallels with those of behavioral interventions as well as direct implications for clinical efficacy. The most widely used stimulant medications, MPH and DEX, have half-lives that are quite short. MPH's half-life is approximately 3.5 hours, with somewhat longer periods for dextroamphetamine. Clinically, the child must therefore receive both a morning and a noon dose in order to be actively medicated during school hours; even then, effects of the medication will typically have worn off by late afternoon. Sustained release preparations of these stimulants (Ritalin-SR, Dexedrine spansules) are often prescribed to avoid the noon dosing regimen (e.g., Fitzpatrick, Klorman, Brumaghim, & Borgstedt, 1992), and the chief rationale for using the alternate stimulant agent pemoline is its longer half-life, requiring one dose per day.

Why is the information regarding time course important? First and foremost, there is no evidence that the behavioral improvements that pertain to medicated periods persist once the active pharmacologic ingredients have dissipated. Thus benefits from time on medication are extremely short-lived. Also, as noted above, the medications have typically worn off by late afternoon, but because of side effects related to eating and sleeping patterns (see below), the medications are not often prescribed for evening hours. Furthermore, weekend usage is not always indicated. Thus medications are likely to have worn off by the very times that are critical for the child's social interactions with parents and peers. Whereas the short duration of stimulant effects is helpful for acute crossover investigations, it is an issue of major clinical concern.

Clinical Benefits of
Stimulant Treatment

As noted above, the stimulants currently in use for ADHD provide benefit for core symptoms in a clear majority of treated youngsters, with positive response rates estimated to range from 60% to 90%.[3] In laboratory and clinic investigations as well as observational studies, important improvements in attention and impulse control and reduction of overactivity have been documented. A central question, however, is whether stimulants effect improvement in those domains related to long-term course. First, stimulants not only reduce generally noncompliant and disruptive behavior but also effect reductions in aggression, with levels of physically and verbally aggressive behavior during active medication periods reduced to the normal range (see review in Hinshaw, 1991). Importantly, such benefits do not typically come at the expense of general reduction of social interaction, attesting to the specificity of the stimulant effects.[4] Furthermore, recent evidence also suggests that stimulants decrease important covert antisocial behaviors like stealing and property destruction (Hinshaw, Heller, & McHale, 1992; see Figure 6.1). Recall, however, that severe aggression and antisocial behavior are typically embedded in complex networks of familial and neighborhood influences; pharmacologic treatments alone, which are directed solely towards individual behavior change, are not likely to alter the course of antisocial activity in children with comorbid ADHD and aggressive behavior unless concentrated intervention is directed towards systemic factors. Thus multimodal intervention strategies are indicated (see subsequent section).

Despite the importance of aggression in mediating peer rejection (Erhardt & Hinshaw, 1993), reductions in aggressive behavior may not necessarily lead to normalization of the peer status of ADHD children. That is, although medication does lead to significant improvement in sociometric status, gains are typically not of sufficient magnitude to bring peer appraisal into the normal range (Whalen et al., 1989). Given the

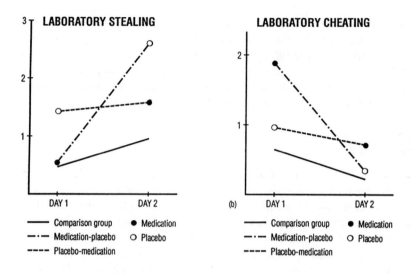

Figure 6.1. Laboratory Stealing and Cheating Scores by Medication (0.3 mg/kg MPH) Order and by Day

SOURCE: Hinshaw, S. P., Heller, T., & McHale, J. P. (1992). Covert antisocial behavior in boys with attention-deficit hyperactivity disorder: External validation and effects of methylphenidate. *Journal of Consulting and Clinical Psychology, 60,* p. 279. Copyright 1992 by the American Psychological Association. Reprinted by permission.

central importance of acceptance by agemates as a predictor of long-term functioning (see Chapter 1), such results should temper enthusiasm for medications as a sole intervention. Adjunctive interventions may be of particular importance for enhancing social performance and peer relationships (Hinshaw, 1992c).

Considerable controversy has been generated with respect to the effects of stimulant medications on academic performance. Because medication rarely leads to improvements in actual achievement test scores, this treatment modality has been criticized as fostering improved behavior at the expense of actual gains in learning (O'Leary, 1980). In the classic report of Sprague and Sleator (1977), the stimulant dosage (1.0 mg/kg MPH) that optimally facilitated behavioral improvement did not lead to any gains relative to placebo regarding a laboratory memory task; the low dosage that enhanced memory performance produced only slight behavioral improvement. Investigations of cognitive and academic performance, however, contain a host of methodologic problems, including inadequately sensitive dependent measures, improper medication dosage levels, and the restricted time course of stimulant actions (Pelham, 1986). More recent investigations, in fact, reveal linear dose response curves for social behavior *and* a variety of indices of academic performance and learning through moderate dosage levels (see Pelham, Bender, Caddell, Booth, & Moorer, 1985). Thus even though achievement scores themselves may be resistant to change in all but extremely lengthy trials, such important outcomes as accuracy of daily academic work are fostered with medication. Furthermore, stimulant effects on problem solving and academic performance are not limited to rote, tedious tasks but pertain also to complex problem solving (e.g., Douglas, Barr, Amin, O'Neill, & Britton, 1988). Indeed medication effects on achievement appear clinically significant in some instances (Kupietz, Winsberg, Richardson, Maitinsky, & Mendell, 1988).

In recent reports, however, Rapport, DuPaul, and Denny (1993) and Swanson, Cantwell, Lerner, McBurnett, and Hanna (1991) have again shown that, for many children, "cognitive toxicity" with respect to learning or achievement may appear at the same dosages that facilitate behavioral improvement. Measures of actual academic performance are therefore crucial adjuncts to medication assessments; theoretically, the field must continue to grapple with some apparent dissociation of behavioral and cognitive effects of stimulants.

In short, stimulant medications effect important, short-term gains not only in the core symptomatology of ADHD but in such critical areas as aggression and antisocial behavior, where normalization of behavior is likely; peer standing, for which effects appear to be of smaller magnitude, lacking clinical significance; and a number of measures of academic performance, short of actual gains in achievement test scores. Research in recent years has broadened the spectrum of domains in which positive medication effects are found (e.g., medication enhances motivation and persistence in the face of failure; Milich, Carlson, Pelham, & Licht, 1991). Furthermore, individual differences in medication response cannot be overstated.

For most youngsters, however, medication treatments fail to produce clinically sufficient benefits across the child's core target problems (Pelham & Hinshaw, 1992).[5] Perhaps most important of all, there is no evidence to date that stimulants alter the course of children with ADHD, even those who appear to be successfully treated in childhood (e.g., Weiss & Hechtman, 1986). Despite some domains of long-term benefit, discontinuity between short-range gains and fundamental long-term improvement is apparent. This key issue of long-term efficacy bears further examination. First, for a host of practical and ethical reasons, no study (as of yet) has randomly assigned ADHD children to long-term regimens of medication versus placebo. All negative long-term results to date are therefore generated from quasi-experiments, and inferences should be made with caution. It is conceivable, for example, that medicated youngsters display more severe initial symptomatology than those not selected for treatment, a clear confounding factor.

Second, in the long-term reports that have emerged, compliance with medication regimens is unknown; in short-term studies, adherence rates are disappointingly low (Firestone, 1982). Third, as indicated earlier, if ADHD is a chronic disorder and if medication effects are extremely short-lived, benefits of stimulant treatment delivered even across several years in childhood may not alter prognosis. In other words, effective interventions (pharmacologic or psychosocial) may require far longer trials than are typically performed; the field may need to reexamine the "acute disorder" model upon which most childhood services are delivered (Kazdin, 1987).[6]

Side Effects

Stimulants tend to suppress appetite, and they may also disrupt sleep patterns. Along with headaches and stomachaches, these side effects are the most commonly reported during trials of stimulants for children with ADHD (Barkley, McMurray, Edelbrock, & Robbins, 1990). In addition, stimulants accelerate heart rate by several beats per minute; but long-term cardiovascular effects have not been noted. As with all other response domains, side effects show great individual variability, and few are of sufficient severity to warrant discontinuation of medication. Furthermore, the study of Barkley, McMurray, Edelbrock, and Robbins (1990) revealed a rather high frequency of "side effects" from parental reports when ADHD children received placebo medication. Nonetheless treatment emergent symptoms (TES), as they are sometimes called, can be bothersome and must be carefully monitored.

Potentially more problematic are the tics—involuntary motor and vocal behaviors—that may accompany stimulant regimens. In many cases, lowering of the medication dosage may halt transient tics; yet in some cases, stimulants apparently speed the display of the chronic motor and vocal tics associated with Tourette's disorder. Slight growth decrements may accrue to long-term, high-dose treatments, but medication holidays during weekends or summers may temper such effects. Finally, media reports of highly unusual, idiosyncratic responses to stimulants (e.g., violence, suicide) appear vanishingly rare and may relate to inappropriate treatment with stimulants of individuals at risk for psychosis. In short, side effects require monitoring, but stimulants actually appear to be among the safest medications prescribed for children.[7]

Do children treated with stimulants begin to attribute their positive behavior to external agents like pills rather than their own effort? Whalen and Henker (1976) initially raised the issue of such psychological "side effects" of stimulant treatment. Recently, however, Pelham, Murphy, et al. (1992) demonstrated that ADHD children attending a summer treatment program not only behaved better while on active medication—and not only made more accurate appraisals of such improvement—but also tended to attribute their improved behavior to personal effort. Discussion of the fascinating issues related to the optimal attributions that should be made by children with psychological and behavioral difficulties is beyond the scope of this chapter.

Alternative Pharmacologic Agents

Space permits only the briefest coverage of this important area. Most important, investigations in the past 5 years report impressive gains for ADHD youngsters who are treated with tricyclic antidepressant medications, particularly desipramine (see Biederman, Baldessarini, Wright, Knee, & Harmatz, 1989). Interestingly, despite the noteworthy gains in important symptom areas, such medications do not produce large improvements in attentional performance per se; they also may be less helpful for ADHD youngsters with comorbid aggression. The positive effects of such medications on ADHD youngsters do not imply that the children have an underlying depression. Indeed, (a) the time course of positive response is quicker than typical antidepressant actions, (b) actual childhood depression is unresponsive to antidepressant effects, and (c) antidepressants produce benefits for other conditions that do not necessarily betray an underlying depression (e.g., migraine headache, enuresis). The neurotransmitter systems influenced by antidepressant medications (serotonin, norepinephrine) subserve multiple areas of the brain, with different behavioral effects. Despite some potentially troublesome side effects, tricyclic and even newer generation antidepressants have gained status as a second-tier treatment option following the stimulants. Other pharmacologic options (e.g., clonidine, antipsychotic agents) are far down the list of potential options (for a helpful diagram of pharmacologic options, see McCracken, 1991).

Summary

Despite the lack of a coherent underlying theoretical justification, stimulant medications are widely used, typically safe, and quite efficacious in the short run for most ADHD youngsters. Recent investigations document that they produce benefits in key problem areas such as aggressive/antisocial behavior and academic productivity, bespeaking their importance in developmentally relevant domains. Yet gains in peer acceptance and actual achievement tend to fall short of clinical significance; furthermore, their extremely short-acting nature precludes their utility for key family and peer interactions. In addition, medication as a sole intervention rarely leads to clinically sufficient gains. Critically, although a definitive trial has yet to be performed, stimulants do not appear to effect long-term change in the course of ADHD. Of extreme importance, therefore, is careful examination of psychosocial treatment options, which may serve as alternatives or adjuncts to pharmacologic intervention strategies.

BEHAVIORAL INTERVENTION FOR ADHD

Principles of operant conditioning began to be applied systematically to externalizing problems of childhood in the 1960s, with a mushrooming of explicit applications to attention deficits and hyperactivity in the 1970s. The movement to behavioral intervention followed decades of a predominantly psychoanalytic formulation of children's behavioral/ emotional problems and a psychodynamic approach to treatment, in which children were seen individually in expressive psychotherapy with the goal of uncovering psychic conflicts (see Chapter 1). Operant formulations, on the other hand, assume that maladaptive behaviors are shaped by faulty environmental contingencies, alteration of which can lead to reductions in problem behavior and replacement with more constructive alternatives. Intervention is therefore apt be performed by parents and teachers, who learn to promote on-task behavior and compliance and to decrease intrusive, disinhibited behaviors through alteration of antecedents and consequences. Systematic reward programs, as well as clear contingencies for misbehavior, are key features of behavioral programs for youngsters with ADHD (see Barkley, 1987). A central assumption of behavioral intervention is that direct modification of behavior is a worthwhile goal; few inferences are made with regard to the symbolic meaning of behavior as indicative of unconscious conflict.

Despite clear gains in important outcomes that were found to accrue to behavioral programs, concerns with the generalization and maintenance of treatment gains led, in the late 1970s and 1980s, to increasing research on so-called cognitive-behavior modification procedures for children with ADHD (e.g., Meichenbaum, 1977). In these formulations, cognitive processes related to problem solving are the targets for behavioral intervention, with the goals of fostering intrinsic motivation and of enabling the child to take control of goal setting and reinforcement. As will be seen, however, cognitive procedures, particularly those related to self-instructional training, have fared quite poorly for children with ADHD.

Although few estimates have been made of the prevalence of behavioral intervention for youngsters with attention deficits and hyperactivity, Copeland, Wolraich, Lindgren, and Milich (1987) showed that behavior modification programs have, in fact, become quite widely used. Several factors—the insistence on empirical data of behavioral investigators, increased awareness of the potential power of behavioral interventions, and enhanced training of practitioners in behavioral strategies—have led to a marked increase in the utilization of such services over the past 2 decades.

Following the structure of Hinshaw and Erhardt (1993) and Pelham and Hinshaw (1992), I divide the wide range of behavioral treatments into three classes for the present discussion: (a) direct contingency management, (b) clinical behavior therapy, and (c) cognitive-behavioral procedures. In describing each class of intervention, I present both positive empirical results and limitations of the particular modality. Throughout, I discuss general issues regarding the implementation of behavioral programs for youngsters with ADHD, pointing out unexpected parallels with medication treatments. Following this section on behavioral intervention, I focus on the possibility for combining pharmacologic and behavioral interventions to effect more lasting gains for the troubling problems of children with attention deficits and hyperactivity.

Direct Contingency Management

The behavioral procedures producing the most immediate and powerful behavior changes for youngsters with ADHD involve direct modification of contingencies in classroom settings. As reviewed in Hinshaw and Erhardt (1993), such direct contingency management typically involves the intentional implementation of a powerful reinforcement system, with clear guidelines for behaviors that both earn and lose points. The latter types of contingencies exemplify response cost procedures, which, along with other prudent negative consequences, may be particularly helpful for children with the kinds of disinhibitory problems related to ADHD (Rapport, Murphy, & Bailey, 1982; Rosen, O'Leary, Joyce, Conway, & Pfiffner, 1984; Sullivan & O'Leary, 1989). I am not advocating uniformly negative or punitive procedures for such youngsters: All behavioral programs must provide a high ratio of positive to negative consequences. Yet mild punishments like response cost and time-out are often crucial additions to behavioral programs for youngsters with attention deficits and hyperactivity.

Most programs involving direct contingency management take the form of demonstration classrooms or other comprehensively programmed environments (e.g., Robinson, Newby, & Ganzell, 1981). Within such comprehensive systems, contingencies can be individualized for a given child. Indeed, a hallmark of effective behavioral programs is their ability to be tailored to the specific profile of behavioral excesses and deficits identified by baseline assessments.

Direct contingency management programs have been shown to effect clinically significant improvements in children with a range of behavioral disorders as well as those diagnosed specifically with ADHD (Pelham et al., 1993; Robinson et al., 1981). Marked increases in academic productivity and efficiency, as well as decreases in disinhibited and disruptive behavior, have been documented, although the average magnitude of gains may not be as strong as those from stimulant medications (Pelham et al., 1993). The same features that make these types of programs so powerful, however, may also serve as their chief limitations. That is, the elaborate nature of the contingency planning and the salience of the continuously delivered external reinforcers are not only costly but are also likely to be quite discontinuous with the child's typical rewards and punishments. The generalizability and maintenance of the improved behavior are therefore of central concern with direct contingency management programs. So long as contingencies are in effect, gains are typically sustained; but as with stimulant medications, there is little evidence for the persistence of improvements when the active ingredient—in this case, the systematic contingency plan—has stopped. Modifications of direct contingency management programs could therefore involve the placing of a trained teacher's aide in the classroom of a child with ADHD, supervised by a consulting teacher (Swanson, 1992).

Clinical Behavior Therapy

By far the most prevalent type of behavioral program for youngsters with ADHD involves a clinic-based set of procedures in which professionals provide individual or group consultation in pertinent strategies to the key adults—parents and teachers—who interact with the child on a daily basis. The goal is to modify the child's everyday environment, promoting behavioral gains in those settings in which problematic behavior typically occurs.

In these types of programs, parents are trained in such strategies as giving positive attention to the child, observing target behaviors, instituting reward/response cost programs, and performing consistent, nonphysical punishments like time-out (see Barkley, 1987; Pelham, Schnedler, Bologna, & Contreras, 1980). Teachers learn similar principles, with an emphasis on developing specific behavioral and academic goals for the child and providing clear consequences for both positive and negative behavior. Furthermore, through joint consultation with families and teachers, incentive systems like daily report card programs that can bridge home and school are planned. A daily report card is a rating sheet on which teachers award points or provide "checks" for the child's meeting of individualized behavioral or academic goals; when the child brings home the sheet each day, parents provide praise and rewards for the child's successful meeting of the goals. The overall principle is to foster consistency between home and school. Typically, the child is not included in the therapeutic contacts of clinical behavior therapy, except to provide consultation about desired reinforcers or, in the case of adolescents, to participate actively in contracting.

Clinical behavior therapy has been evaluated, with ADHD children, in reports involving single-case experimental methodology as well as in group comparison designs. Clinically significant benefits have been shown, over periods of several months, for rated and observed symptomatology, aggression in classrooms, parent-child interaction, and some measures of academic performance (e.g., Abikoff & Gittelman, 1984;

Pisterman et al., 1989). A further advantage of clinical behavior therapy procedures includes their ability to provide clinical benefit for those time periods during which stimulant medication is inactive. That is, when medications have worn off in the evening, the family can continue with behavioral programming.

Regarding magnitude of benefits, the finding of Pelham et al. (1980) is particularly noteworthy: Three months of intensive clinical behavior therapy yielded change in classroom behavior that was intermediate between the levels induced by low and moderate dosages of MPH. Yet for most dependent measures, clinical behavior therapy programs fail to produce normalized functioning, particularly for peer relations (Pelham & Hinshaw, 1992). In addition, head-to-head comparisons often favor stimulant medications for short-term behavior change (Gittelman et al., 1980). Furthermore, clinical behavior therapy is not an easy treatment to implement, given its demands on parent and teacher time. Note also that evaluation is often problematic, in that participating parents and teachers obviously cannot be "blind" to treatment conditions. In short, clinical behavior therapy programs have documented efficacy, but they appear insufficient.

Cognitive-Behavioral Procedures

Because of the detail available in relatively recent reviews (Abikoff, 1991; Hinshaw & Erhardt, 1991), consideration of cognitive-behavioral procedures will be brief. These treatments are, in some respects, more traditional than other behavioral strategies, in that the goals are to teach problem solving and verbal mediation skills in individual or small-group therapy models. Thus the child is the direct client of the therapist. Considerable promise was initially held for such therapeutic strategies, particularly with respect to the potential for generalization and maintenance. That is, the child would allegedly learn to set performance goals, monitor behavior, and provide self-reinforcement or error-correction strategies without the need for external contingency systems. The heart of such procedures, in most applications, involves self-instructional training, whereby the therapist initially directs the child's task performance through spoken directives and then transfers such control to the child's internalized speech. This procedure was designed to remediate alleged deficits in verbal mediation skills (Meichenbaum, 1977).

Results of clinical trials based on self-instruction-based cognitive therapy have, however, been dismal (e.g., Abikoff & Gittelman, 1985).

This state of affairs is particularly striking given the positive results of cognitive-behavioral, problem-solving therapies in young children with aggression (Kazdin, Bass, Siegel, & Thomas, 1989). Why are such procedures apparently ineffective for children with ADHD? First, it is conceivable that the premise upon which most cognitive-behavioral programing is based—namely, that teaching self-instructional skills will compensate for ADHD children's deficits in verbal mediation—is misguided. Even if verbal mediation deficits are operative in some youngsters with ADHD (Berk & Potts, 1991), it is questionable whether training the child to recapitulate the putative developmental sequence—from control by adult directions to internalized speech—is therapeutic. The few positive outcomes of cognitive-behavioral treatment for ADHD children do not involve self-instructional intervention but instead focus on blends of cognitive problem solving and reinforced behavioral rehearsal to effect increases in self-monitoring skills and anger management (Hinshaw, Buhrmester, & Heller, 1989; Hinshaw, Henker, & Whalen, 1984a, 1984b).

Second, developmental factors may not be given sufficient weight with such treatments. Perhaps ADHD youngsters of elementary-school age lack the cognitive sophistication to alter fundamental problem-solving strategies. In addition, children with comorbid ADHD and aggression—the group most likely to be referred for treatment—may be particularly resistant to all but the most powerful interventions, given the constellation of cognitive, neuropsychological, and peer-related difficulties that accrue to this group (Hinshaw & Erhardt, 1991). Finally, given current theorizing regarding the fundamental role of disinhibitory processes in ADHD (see Chapter 3), the ideal sequence of treatment may be to foster enhanced behavioral control via extrinsic reinforcement procedures and then to employ cognitive-behavioral self-management therapies to promote generalized and durable gains (W. Pelham, personal communication, September, 1992). In other words, the extreme dyscontrol exhibited by children with attention deficits and hyperactivity may not yield to initial treatment that is directed chiefly at cognitions; once behavior is more manageable, however, problem solving strategies may be invoked to extend benefits. In all, cognitive-behavioral procedures are quite unlikely to be beneficial on their own for the difficult problems of ADHD; their combination with reinforcement contingencies to extend the benefits of reinforcement-based interventions has not received adequate evaluation.

Summary

Behavior therapy procedures, particularly those involving direct contingency management or comprehensive clinical behavior therapy, have been shown to provide clear benefits for youngsters with ADHD. Although head-to-head comparisons with stimulant medications often favor the latter intervention (Gittelman et al., 1980; Pelham et al., 1993), behavioral procedures have produced important changes in social behavior and classroom performance. Yet many of the same limitations that were noted for pharmacologic treatments also pertain to behavioral intervention. For one thing, the response rate is not universal, with a key factor involving the demands placed on parents and teachers to alter expectations, environments, and their own behavior. Teachers may refuse to comply, and isolated families in lower socioeconomic strata may have particular difficulties in following through. Second, gains from behavioral programs are typically not sufficient to bring the child into normal ranges of functioning across all important outcome domains (Pelham & Hinshaw, 1992). Third, effects of behavioral intervention typically terminate when contingencies are lifted; like gains from medication, effects fail to persist when intervention stops. Such failure to attain lasting treatment gains is probably the most important limitation of this class of intervention.

In short, the most effective treatments researched to date—stimulant medications and the large class of behavioral programs—share similar drawbacks, the most salient of which is their inability to yield clinically sufficient or durable gains when used singly.[8] The pertinent question is whether intervention combinations can address such deficiencies and promote more lasting benefits.

TREATMENT COMBINATIONS

From a theoretical perspective, two different classes of intervention for a given disorder could combine in several ways (see Uhlenhuth, Lipman, & Covi, 1969). (a) Their effects might summate, producing additive benefit for a particular domain. (b) Alternatively, they could interact synergistically, so that the effects of the joint intervention would be greater than the sum of the parts. On the other hand, (c) reciprocal effects could accrue, in which benefits from the combination would be no greater than those from a single modality. (d) In some cases, negative effects could result; the combination might counteract the effects of the sole treatments. Each of these possibilities pertains to joint treatment effects on a given outcome domain. For ADHD, however, several target areas are often clinically salient. Thus (e) effects might be complementary, meaning that one treatment would produce change in certain outcome domains, with the alternate intervention effecting benefit for different dependent measures. What happens when behavioral and pharmacologic treatment strategies are combined for children with ADHD?

In their seminal review, Pelham and Murphy (1986) systematically appraised the extant intervention reports that addressed intervention combinations for ADHD. Although a majority of the investigations in this review suggested at least additive effects of pharmacologic-psychosocial treatment combinations, (a) the total number of subjects evaluated was rather small; (b) most of the behavioral interventions were of short duration; (c) some behavioral-spectrum treatments (e.g., cognitive therapies) failed to yield benefits on their own, obviously limiting their potential for effecting combined efficacy; and (d) outcome measures varied widely in scope, reliability, and ecological validity. Furthermore, whereas the treatment combinations in many of these reports were ranked ahead of the single interventions with regard to key outcomes, they often did not show statistically significant increments over the sole treatments. In addition, the last half of the 1980s witnessed a marked slowing of comparative and combination treatment designs for children with ADHD, chiefly because of the logistic and economic problems associated with mounting the types of studies necessary to yield data on relative efficacy of treatment combinations over long time periods (Hinshaw & Erhardt, 1993). Fortunately, in recent years several major combination trials have been mounted, which promise to provide more definitive answers to questions of combined efficacy (see below). Although exhaustive coverage of the relevant data base is outside the scope of this chapter, highlights of several key investigations may prove heuristic.

First, in the authoritative combination trial of Gittelman et al. (1980), 2 months of intensive clinical behavior therapy were not as productive as relatively high dosage levels of individually titrated MPH for the key outcomes of adult ratings and behavior observations. In addition, reciprocation appeared to apply to the combination of behavior therapy and medication, in that this joint treatment did not provide significantly greater benefit than did pharmacologic treatment alone. Yet only this combination treatment produced gains that brought children's rated and observed classroom behavior into the normal range, suggesting some incremental benefit. Second, the within-subject investigation of Pelham et al. (1980), discussed earlier, showed that 3 months of intensive clinical behavior therapy reduced the stimulant dosage required by many of the participating ADHD youngsters. As argued in Pelham and Hinshaw (1992), combining the two classes of intervention may allow reductions in the dosage or intensity level of both medication (which could prevent the display of key side effects) and of psychosocial treatment—for example, clinical behavior therapy could be substituted for intensive, classroom-based contingency management.

Third, individual differences in response to combined medication-behavioral interventions must be carefully monitored because different youngsters show positive response to different components of intervention or to different levels of intensity of combinations (Pelham et al., 1993). For example, careful individual evaluations suggest that some youngsters will respond to behavioral treatments without need for medications; yet unless parents and teachers work carefully to promote generalization of initial gains, effects of psychosocial intervention will dissipate. Finally, as discussed in Pelham and Hinshaw (1992), the most salient treatment effect from behavioral-medication combinations may be complementarity: the selective benefits of different modalities for different domains of functioning. For instance, medications may yield benefits on classroom attention that no additional treatment can increment. Yet, at home, the important area of parent-child interaction may be relatively unaffected by pharmacologic treatment, given the short half-life of stimulants; and behavioral family treatment may exert important effects on this domain, complementing the daytime effects of the pharmacologic agents. The potential for knowledge of even wider complementarity may be limited primarily by our inability to monitor treatment outcome in multiple domains of functioning (e.g., peer relations, academic achievement, self-concept) in the same investigation.

The major limitation of extant multicomponent treatment investigations is their relatively short-term focus. Indeed, a "long" intervention within the current literature would be one extending for a period of several months—a time period that is clearly inadequate to contend with the many areas in which ADHD youngsters display deficiencies. Conceivably, discontinuity exists between the types of treatment that are optimal for producing short-term improvements in children with ADHD and those that could yield long-term change. In the literature on adult obesity, for example, the quickest effects on weight reduction are typically found with pharmacologic treatments (which, interestingly, are likely to be variants of stimulant medications). Yet although medication may produce greater short-term benefits than does behavioral treatment for weight control—particularly when given as the initial treatment—it may yield greater rates of relapse than does behavioral intervention alone (see Rodin, Elias, Silberstein, & Wagner, 1988). Whereas adult obesity and childhood ADHD obviously differ in important ways, the point is that different mechanisms may subserve short- versus long-term treatment efficacy. Without protracted intervention strategies and without long-range follow-up, attempts to generalize from the results of short-term trials could be misguided.

An exception to the short-range nature of treatment investigations for ADHD is the groundbreaking multimodality intervention study of Satterfield and colleagues at UCLA. The goal in this trial was to provide long-term, individually tailored treatments to youngsters with (at that time) hyperactivity, in an attempt to effect lasting change in academic, social, family-related, and behavioral outcome domains. The participating children and families received, on the basis of an individual assessment plan, any or all of a number of component treatments, including stimulant medication, tutoring, individual child therapy, parent management groups, or marital therapy. Results indicated, at follow-up periods of 1 to 3 years following the intensive treatment, outcomes that were better than expected on the basis of normative data for hyperactive youngsters (e.g., Satterfield, Cantwell, & Satterfield, 1979; Satterfield, Satterfield, & Cantwell, 1981). Furthermore, for youngsters participating in the full range of multimodality treatments, rates of delinquency during adolescence were markedly reduced (Satterfield, Satterfield, & Schell, 1987).

Yet key methodologic issues prevent enthusiastic acceptance of these findings. Because the investigation was not experimental—no random assignment to treatment groups occurred, and no nontreated comparison group was employed—inferences of improvement to the treatments per se must be made cautiously. Furthermore, no precise algorithm specified the precise treatment components that were delivered to each child; and the large attrition rates at follow-up evaluations (fewer than 50% of the sample were available at 3-year follow-up) may well signify that only the most motivated families persevered through the intervention and follow-up periods. These critiques point out the difficult logistic and methodologic issues involved in the attempt to ascertain the benefits of long-term multimodal treatments. As explicated by Whalen and Henker (1991), investigations designed to contrast differing treatments or to evaluate combined efficacy are fraught with conceptual problems. Nonetheless, the stakes are high for youngsters with ADHD and their families. An essential need is obtaining valid information relevant to the types of treatment, delivered over lengthy time periods, that can alter the course of the disorder for various subgroups.

NIMH MULTIMODAL TREATMENT STUDY
FOR CHILDREN WITH ADHD

In recent years the National Institute of Mental Health (NIMH) has funded several multicomponent treatment studies for children with ADHD, most notably the intensive kindergarten intervention of Russell Barkley in Massachusetts and the pharmacologic-behavioral combination study of Howard Abikoff in New York and Lily Hechtman in Montreal. Both studies involve multipronged treatment for a full year, with booster intervention for an additional year-long period. Although results from these trials are not yet available, their funding and implementation signal a serious commitment to large-scale comparative and combination intervention trials. The Child and Adolescent Disorders Research Branch of NIMH has laid the groundwork in the past year for a multisite investigation that promises to be the most intensive and lengthiest treatment study to date.

The premises of this collaborative venture are several: ADHD engenders substantial risk for a negative course; it is a heterogeneous condition, involving substantial comorbidity with other disorders; sample sizes and resources at any one site are likely to be insufficient to evaluate treatment effects with sufficient power or to ascertain interactions of subject characteristics with intervention response; and extant treatment studies evaluating intervention combinations have either been short-term in nature or uncontrolled experimentally (Richters et al., 1993). In soliciting applications to participate in the collaborative treatment protocol, NIMH therefore specified that designs include comparisons and combinations of psychosocial and pharmacologic treatments conducted over relatively long time periods (2 years) and that investigators be willing to collaborate with other sites, so that a sufficient overall sample size could be obtained.[9]

Each site is to recruit and screen 96 children meeting extensive criteria for ADHD, with random assignment to one of four treatment conditions: (a) stimulant medication, (b) intensive psychosocial intervention,

(c) medication-psychosocial treatments combined, or (d) community comparison. Medication treatments will involve a preliminary trial to ascertain optimal dose before a long maintenance phase is instituted; psychosocial interventions are predicated on the principles of intensity and generalization and will include systematic family, educational, and child components. The goals are to ascertain the separate and combined effects of well-delivered, state-of-the-art pharmacologic and psychosocial treatments for a wide range of youngsters with ADHD and to assess their benefits over and above the typical interventions received in the community. Planning for this intensive investigation is ongoing at the time of writing this chapter, with the goal of devising a common assessment and treatment protocol so that data can be amalgamated across sites. In addition to addressing questions of relative and combined efficacy of psychosocial and pharmacologic treatments, the hope is that important secondary issues related to subgroup response, mechanisms of treatment, and predictors of long-term outcome can be answered.

FINAL THOUGHTS

Despite the intensity of these planned interventions for the multisite investigation, the prospect of altering the course of ADHD is a sobering one. The ADHD youngsters most likely to escalate into an antisocial outcome appear to be those with comorbid aggression, and such youth tend to have parents with antisocial behavior patterns. Treatment adherence is known to be difficult for such multiproblem families, who often lack the motivation, financial resources, or organization necessary to respond to intervention. In addition, treatment will need to address the effects of deviant peer cultures on aggressive ADHD youngsters, given that such peer influence is particularly likely for children with poor family monitoring—the typical state of affairs for youth on an antisocial trajectory. Such issues and problems are likely to supplement the well-documented problems of ADHD children in academic achievement and behavioral disinhibition, challenging traditional intervention paradigms.

These concerns, however, are quite different from those pertaining to the group of children displaying attention deficits without hyperactivity (ADD/WO). Such youngsters are likely to display sluggishness, language delays, and internalizing problems, which present different but equally daunting challenges to interventionists. As I have highlighted throughout the book, the great variability among children who receive diagnoses of ADHD must be confronted by those interested in classification, nosology, and etiology as well as treatment. Whether continued research on underlying mechanisms can help to illuminate such variability—and whether it can inform the development of interventions that might fundamentally alter the course of this variegated disorder—will be the subject of future books on attention deficits and hyperactivity in children.

NOTES

1. Although space limitations preclude extended discussion of preventive interventions for attention deficits and hyperactivity, a similar focus on underlying mechanisms of transmission should foster improved prevention efforts as well. For instance, improved understanding of the attentional or disinhibitory sequelae of even moderate amounts of alcohol, tobacco, or illicit substance use in pregnancy may precipitate renewed preventive strategies. At a different level, efforts aimed at the enhancement of parenting skill, which could prevent the development of secondary aggression in youngsters who are at risk for attention problems and disinhibition, may be of critical importance. Implementation of parent education among the general population, however, presents formidable ethical and logistic hurdles.

2. Several misconceptions about stimulants bear brief comment. First, despite repeated assertions to the contrary, these medications do not act paradoxically to "calm" hyperactive youngsters but appear to have effects on nondiagnosed children and normal adults that are quite similar to those for youngsters with ADHD (Rapoport et al., 1978). Such effects are presumably related to the enhancement of dimensions of self-regulation and attention across all individuals, mediated via actions on dopamine, norepinephrine, and epinephrine in key central and peripheral sites (e.g., McCracken, 1991; Zametkin & Rapoport, 1987). Second, positive response to a stimulant does not, as a result, validate a diagnosis of ADHD. Children of other diagnostic groups may also display enhanced attention and behavior with stimulant medications (Brown, Jaffe, Silverstein, & Magee, 1991).

3. I must comment that it appears inappropriate to classify ADHD children globally as "responders" or "nonresponders" to stimulants. Not only are medication effects quite idiosyncratic across children, but even in the same child, different behavioral domains may yield divergent responses (Rapport et al., 1988). This point is crucial in evaluating the pharmacologic literature. For example, dose-response relationships that are averaged across children may apply to only a handful of the individuals involved. Individualized monitoring of medication response across several disparate domains of functioning is therefore essential for scientific as well as clinical reasons.

4. Pelham and Bender (1982) have shown, however, that for some youngsters with ADHD, particularly those with initially low rates of negative social behavior, treatment with stimulants may suppress all social interaction in dramatic fashion. Individual differences in medication response must always be considered.

5. Space permits only brief mention regarding the important issue of which factors predict stimulant response. Despite heroic efforts over the years to ascertain the variables

that forecast a positive outcome during a course of stimulant treatment, few robust predictors have emerged. Indeed, given the high rates of positive response for most outcome measures, such a state of affairs may be expected on statistical grounds alone. Taylor et al. (1987) found that inattentive/restless behaviors, but not defiance, predicted a positive response to MPH, as did a narrow diagnosis of hyperkinesis as opposed to more lenient American diagnostic criteria. Also, regarding subtypes (see Chapter 5), Barkley, DuPaul, and McMurray (1990) found that ADD/WO youngsters displayed a greater likelihood of adverse response to MPH than did ADD/H children; overall, the former group responded to lower dosage levels. In addition, perhaps the most robust finding in the field is that the concurrent presence of anxiety or other internalizing symptoms predicts a negative response to stimulant medications (Barkley, DuPaul, & McMurray, 1990; Pliszka, 1989; Taylor et al., 1987; see also Chapter 5). Pliszka (1987) believes that comorbid internalizing symptomatology predicts preferential response to antidepressant intervention.

6. In fact, as the persistent nature of ADHD has received increasing recognition, investigators and practitioners are more willing to extend stimulant treatment into adolescence and even adulthood (e.g., Pelham, Vodde-Hamilton, Murphy, Greenstein, & Vallano, 1991; Wender, Reimherr, Wood, & Ward, 1985). I must point out, however, that positive response rates to stimulant medications appear to be lower for adolescents than for children, with even further declines in successful treatment rates by adulthood. It therefore becomes even more critical to explore adjunctive or alternative interventions for ADHD youngsters as they develop and mature.

7. Stimulants are often contraindicated for children with histories or even family histories of tic or Tourette's disorder. Furthermore, given the abuse potential of stimulant agents for adolescents or adults, these medications should not be prescribed where known drug abuse occurs in the family. Yet successful stimulant treatment does not appear to increase risk for later substance abuse in youngsters with ADHD.

8. Because of limited space, I address alternative interventions to medications and behavioral treatments with the utmost brevity. First, the value of expressive psychotherapies (e.g., play therapy) for ADHD children is under severe question. Although in wide use at child guidance clinics and psychotherapy offices across the United States, such treatments have extremely limited evidence regarding their ability to affect core symptomatology or to enhance academic success, peer relationships, or reductions in aggression. Some investigators, however, contend that expressive therapies may be beneficial for fostering ADHD youngsters' abilities to cope with family conflict or for bolstering self-esteem. Expressive therapies cannot, however, be considered a primary intervention for ADHD. Next, despite considerable interest, the wide array of dietary interventions for attention deficits and hyperactivity lack empirical support (Conners, 1980). Finally, in spite of aggressive marketing in some locales, biofeedback and chiropractic interventions for ADHD are without solid foundation. Regarding the former, some theoretical rationale can be found (Conners & Wells, 1986), but it is difficult to imagine that a solitary, office-based procedure with the goal of altering neurophysiologic indicators could effect durable change in the varied problems exhibited by children with ADHD. Given the intractability of the deficits that comprise this disorder, alternative interventions would be welcome, but the onus is on their advocates to demonstrate meaningful gains.

9. Following peer review in the summer of 1992, the following sites (with principal investigators in parentheses) were selected for participation: Columbia University (Laurence Greenhill), Duke University (C. Keith Conners), Long Island Jewish Medical Center

(Howard Abikoff), University of California—Berkeley (Stephen Hinshaw), University of California—Irvine (James Swanson), and Western Psychiatric Institute and Clinics at the University of Pittsburgh (William Pelham). NIMH serves as the coordinating body for the study (Peter Jensen, Chief, Child and Adolescent Disorders Research Branch).

REFERENCES

Abikoff, H. (1991). Cognitive training in ADHD children: Less to it than meets the eye. *Journal of Learning Disabilities, 24*, 205-209.

Abikoff, H., Courtney, M., Pelham, W., & Koplewicz, H. (in press). Detection bias in teacher ratings of attention-deficit hyperactivity disorder and oppositional defiant disorder. *Journal of Abnormal Child Psychology.*

Abikoff, H., & Gittelman, R. (1984). Does behavior therapy normalize the classroom behavior of hyperactive children? *Archives of General Psychiatry, 41*, 449-454.

Abikoff, H., & Gittelman, R. (1985). Hyperactive children treated with stimulants: Is cognitive therapy a useful adjunct? *Archives of General Psychiatry, 42*, 953-961.

Abikoff, H., Gittelman-Klein, R., & Klein, D. (1977). Validation of a classroom observation code for hyperactive children. *Journal of Consulting and Clinical Psychology, 45*, 772-783.

Achenbach, T. M. (1990). Conceptualization of developmental psychopathology. In M. Lewis & S. M. Miller (Eds.), *Handbook of developmental psychopathology* (pp. 3-14). New York: Plenum.

Achenbach, T. M. (1991). *Manual for the Child Behavior Checklist/4-18 and 1991 Profile.* Burlington: University of Vermont Department of Psychiatry.

Achenbach, T. M., & Edelbrock, C. (1978). The classification of child psychopathology: A review and analysis of empirical efforts. *Psychological Bulletin, 85*, 1275-1301.

Achenbach, T. M., McConaughy, S. H., & Howell, C. T. (1987). Child/adolescent behavioral and emotional problems: Implications of cross-informant correlations for situational specificity. *Psychological Bulletin, 101*, 213-232.

American Psychiatric Association. (1968). *Diagnostic and statistical manual of mental disorders* (2nd ed.). Washington, DC: Author.

American Psychiatric Association. (1980). *Diagnostic and statistical manual of mental disorders* (3rd ed.). Washington, DC: Author.

American Psychiatric Association. (1987). *Diagnostic and statistical manual of mental disorders* (3rd ed., rev.). Washington, DC: Author.

American Psychiatric Association. (1994). *Diagnostic and statistical manual of mental disorders* (4th ed.). Washington, DC: Author.

Anastasi, A. (1988). *Psychological testing* (6th ed.). New York: Macmillan.

Anastopoulos, A. D., Guevremont, D. C., Shelton, T. L., & DuPaul, J. J. (1992). Parenting stress among families of children with attention deficit hyperactivity disorder. *Journal of Abnormal Child Psychology, 20*, 503-520.

Anderson, C. A., Hinshaw, S. P., & Simmel, C. (in press). Mother-child interactions in ADHD and comparison boys: Relationships to overt and covert externalizing behavior. *Journal of Abnormal Child Psychology*.

Anderson, J. C., Williams, S. M., McGee, R. O., & Silva, P. A. (1987). DSM-III disorders in pre-adolescent children. *Archives of General Psychiatry, 44*, 69-76.

Angold, A., Cox, A., Prendergast, M., Rutter, M., & Simonoff, E. (1987). *The Child and Adolescent Psychiatric Assessment (CAPA)*. Unpublished manuscript, Duke University Medical Center.

Asher, S. R., & Coie, J. D. (1990). *Peer rejection in childhood*. New York: Cambridge University Press.

Balthazor, M. J., Wagner, R. K., & Pelham, W. E. (1991). The specificity of the effects of stimulant medication on classroom learning-related measures of cognitive processing for attention deficit disorder children. *Journal of Abnormal Child Psychology, 19*, 35-52.

Barkley, R. A. (1987). *Defiant children: A clinician's manual for parent training*. New York: Guilford.

Barkley, R. A. (1988). Attention-deficit hyperactivity disorder. In E. J. Mash & L. G. Terdal (Eds.), *Assessment of childhood disorders* (2nd ed., pp. 69-104). New York: Guilford.

Barkley, R. A. (1989). The problem of stimulus control and rule-governed behavior in children with attention deficit disorder with hyperactivity. In L. M. Bloomingdale & J. Swanson (Eds.), *Attention deficit disorder* (Vol. 4, pp. 203-228). Oxford, UK: Pergamon.

Barkley, R. A. (1990). *Attention deficit hyperactivity disorder: A handbook for diagnosis and treatment*. New York: Guilford.

Barkley, R. A. (1991). The ecological validity of laboratory and analogue assessment methods of ADHD symptoms. *Journal of Abnormal Child Psychology, 19*, 149-178.

Barkley, R. A. (in press). Impaired delayed responding: A unified theory of attention-deficit hyperactivity disorder. In D. K. Routh (Ed.), *Disruptive behavior disorders in childhood: Essays honoring Herbert C. Quay*. New York: Plenum.

Barkley, R. A., & Cunningham, C. (1979). The effects of methylphenidate on the mother-child interactions of hyperactive children. *Archives of General Psychiatry, 36*, 201-208.

Barkley, R. A., DuPaul, G. J., & McMurray, M. B. (1990). Attention deficit disorder with and without hyperactivity: Clinical response to three dose levels of methylphenidate. *Pediatrics, 87*, 519-531.

Barkley, R. A., Fischer, M., Edelbrock, C. S., & Smallish, L. (1990). The adolescent outcome of hyperactive children diagnosed by research criteria: I. An 8-year prospective follow-up study. *Journal of the American Academy of Child and Adolescent Psychiatry, 29*, 546-557.

Barkley, R. A., Grodzinsky, G., & DuPaul, G. J. (1992). Frontal lobe functions in attention deficit disorder with and without hyperactivity: A review and research report. *Journal of Abnormal Child Psychology, 20*, 163-188.

Barkley, R. A., Guevremont, D., Anastopoulos, A., DuPaul, G., & Shelton, T. (1993). Driving related risks and outcomes of attention deficit hyperactivity disorders in adolescents and young adults: A 3- to 5-year follow-up survey. *Pediatrics, 92*, 212-218.

Barkley, R. A., McMurray, M. B., Edelbrock, C. S., & Robbins, K. (1989). The response of aggressive and nonaggressive ADHD children to two doses of methylphenidate. *Journal of the American Academy of Child and Adolescent Psychiatry, 28*, 873881.

Barkley, R. A., McMurray, M. B., Edelbrock, C. S., & Robbins, K. (1990). Side effects of methylphenidate in children with attention deficit hyperactivity disorder: A systematic, placebo-controlled evaluation. *Pediatrics, 86*, 184-192.

Bauermeister, J. J., Alegria, M., Bird, H., Rubio-Stipec, M., & Canino, G. (1992). Are attentional-hyperactivity deficits unidimensional or multidimensional syndromes? Empirical findings from a community survey. *Journal of the American Academy of Child and Adolescent Psychiatry, 31*, 423-431.

Befera, M. S., & Barkley, R. A. (1985). Hyperactive and normal girls and boys: Mother-child interactions, parent psychiatric status, and child psychopathology. *Journal of Child Psychology and Psychiatry, 26*, 439-452.

Beitchman, J., Hood, J., & Inglis, A. (1990). Psychiatric risk in children with speech and language disorders. *Journal of Abnormal Child Psychology, 18*, 283-296.

Berk, L. E., & Potts, M. (1991). Development and functional significance of private speech among attention-deficit hyperactivity disordered and normal boys. *Journal of Abnormal Child Psychology, 19*, 357-377.

Berry, C. A., Shaywitz, S. E., & Shaywitz, B. A. (1985). Girls with attention deficit disorder: A silent majority? A report on behavioral and cognitive characteristics. *Pediatrics, 76*, 801-809.

Bhatia, M. S., Nigam, V. R., Bohra, N., & Malik, S. C. (1991). Attention deficit disorder with hyperactivity among paediatric outpatients. *Journal of Child Psychology and Psychiatry, 32*, 297-306.

Bickett, L., & Milich, R. (1990). First impressions formed of boys with attention deficit disorder. *Journal of Learning Disabilities, 23*, 253-259.

Biederman, J., Baldessarini, R. J., Wright, V., Knee, D., & Harmatz, J. S. (1989). A double-blind placebo controlled study of desipramine in the treatment of ADD: I. Efficacy. *Journal of the American Academy of Child and Adolescent Psychiatry, 28*, 903-911.

Biederman, J., Faraone, S. V., Keenan, K., Steingard, R., & Tsuang, M. T. (1991). Familial association between attention deficit disorder and anxiety disorders. *American Journal of Psychiatry, 148*, 251-256.

Biederman, J., Faraone, S. V., Keenan, K., & Tsuang, M. T. (1991). Evidence of familial association between attention deficit disorder and major affective disorders. *Archives of General Psychiatry, 48*, 633-642.

Biederman, J., Keenan, K., & Faraone, S. V. (1990). Parent-based diagnosis of attention deficit disorder predicts a diagnosis based on teacher report. *Journal of the American Academy of Child and Adolescent Psychiatry, 29*, 698-701.

Biederman, J., Munir, K., & Knee, D. (1987). Conduct and oppositional disorder in clinically referred children with attention deficit disorder: A controlled family study. *Journal of the American Academy of Child and Adolescent Psychiatry, 26*, 724-727.

Biederman, J., Munir, K., Knee, D., Armentano, M., Autor, S., Waternaux, C., & Tsuang, M. T. (1987). High rate of affective disorders in probands with attention deficit disorder and their relatives: A controlled family study. *American Journal of Psychiatry, 144*, 330-333.

Biederman, J., Newcorn, J., & Sprich, S. (1991). Comorbidity of attention deficit hyperactivity disorder with conduct, depressive, anxiety, and other disorders. *American Journal of Psychiatry, 148*, 564-577.

Bird, H. R., Canino, G., Rubio-Stipec, M., Gould, M. S., Ribera, J., Sesman, M., Woodbury, M., Huertas-Goldman, S., Pagan, A., Sanchez-Lacay, A., & Moscoso, M.

(1988). Estimates of the prevalence of childhood maladjustment in a community survey in Puerto Rico. *Archives of General Psychiatry, 45*, 1120-1126.

Blashfield, R. K. (1984). *The classification of psychopathology: Neo-Kraepelinian and quantitative approaches.* New York: Plenum.

Bradley, C. (1937). The behavior of children receiving benzedrine. *American Journal of Psychiatry, 94*, 577-585.

Breen, M. J., & Altepeter, T. S. (1990). *Disruptive behavior disorders in children: Treatment-focused assessment.* New York: Guilford.

Brown, R. T., Coles, C., Platzman, K., & Hill, L. (1993, February). *Parental alcohol exposure and its relationship to externalizing disorders: A longitudinal investigation.* Paper presented at the annual meeting of the Society for Research in Child and Adolescent Psychopathology, Santa Fe.

Brown, R. T., Jaffe, S. L., Silverstein, J., & Magee, H. (1991). Methylphenidate and adolescents hospitalized with conduct disorder: Dose effects on classroom behavior, academic performance, and impulsivity. *Journal of Clinical Child Psychology, 20*, 282-292.

Campbell, S. B. (1990). *Behavior problems in preschool children.* New York: Guilford.

Campbell, S. B., & Ewing, L. J. (1990). Follow-up of hard-to-manage preschoolers: Adjustment at age 9 and predictors of continuing symptoms. *Journal of Child Psychology and Psychiatry, 31*, 871-889.

Campbell, S. B., March, C. L., Pierce, E. W., Ewing, L. J., & Szumowski, E. K. (1991). Hard-to-manage preschool boys: Family context and the stability of externalizing behavior. *Journal of Abnormal Child Psychology, 19*, 301-318.

Cantwell, D. P. (1975). Genetics of hyperactivity. *Journal of Child Psychology and Psychiatry, 16*, 261-264.

Cantwell, D. P., & Baker, L. (1992). Attention deficit disorder with and without hyperactivity: A review and comparison of matched groups. *Journal of the American Academy of Child and Adolescent Psychiatry, 31*, 432-438.

Cantwell, D. P., & Hanna, G. L. (1989). Attention-deficit hyperactivity disorder. In A. Tasman, R. E. Hales, & A. J. Frances (Eds.), *Review of psychiatry* (pp. 134-161). Washington, DC: American Psychiatric Press.

Carlson, C. L. (1986). Attention deficit disorder without hyperactivity: A review of preliminary experimental evidence. In B. B. Lahey & A. E. Kazdin (Eds.), *Advances in clinical child psychology* (Vol. 9, pp. 153-176). New York: Plenum.

Carlson, C. L., Lahey, B. B., Frame, C. L., Walker, J., & Hynd, G. W. (1987). Sociometric status of clinic-referred children with attention deficit disorder with and without hyperactivity. *Journal of Abnormal Child Psychology, 15*, 537-547.

Caron, C., & Rutter, M. (1991). Comorbidity in child psychopathology: Concepts, issues, and research strategies. *Journal of Child Psychology and Psychiatry, 32*, 1063-1080.

Caspi, A., & Moffitt, T. E. (in press). The continuity of maladaptive behavior. In D. Cicchetti & D. Cohen (Eds.), *Manual of developmental psychopathology.* New York: John Wiley.

Chess, S., & Thomas, A. (1984). *Origins and evolution of behavior disorders.* New York: Brunner/Mazel.

Cicchetti, D., & Richters, J. (1993). Developmental considerations in the investigation of conduct disorder. *Development and Psychopathology, 5*, 331-344.

Clements, S. D. (1966). *Minimal brain dysfunction in children—Terminology and identification.* (USPHS Publication No. 1415). Washington, DC: Government Printing Office.

Cloninger, G. R., Christiansen, C. O., Reich, T., & Gottesman, I. L. (1978). Implications of sex differences in the prevalences of anti-social personality, alcoholism, and criminality for familial transmission. *Archives of General Psychiatry, 35*, 941-951.

Coie, J. D., Dodge, K. A., & Kupersmidt, J. (1990). Peer group behavior and social status. In S. R. Asher & J. D. Coie (Eds.), *Peer rejection in childhood* (pp. 17-59). New York: Cambridge University Press.

Conners, C. K. (1980). *Food additives and hyperactive children.* New York: Plenum.

Conners, C. K., & Wells, K. C. (1986). *Hyperkinetic children: A neuropsychosocial approach.* Beverly Hills, CA: Sage.

Copeland, L., Wolraich, C., Lindgren, S., & Milich, R. (1987). Pediatricians' reported practices in the assessment and treatment of attention deficit disorders. *Journal of Developmental and Behavioral Pediatrics, 8*, 191-197.

Costello, E. J., Loeber, R., & Stouthamer-Loeber, M. (1991). Pervasive and situational hyperactivity—confounding effect of informant: A research note. *Journal of Child Psychology and Psychiatry, 32*, 367-376.

Cowart, V. S. (1988). The Ritalin controversy: What's made this drug's opponents hyperactive? *Journal of the American Medical Association, 259*, 2521-2523.

Douglas, V. I. (1983). Attention and cognitive problems. In M. Rutter (Ed.), *Developmental neuropsychiatry* (pp. 280-329). New York: Guilford.

Douglas, V. I., Barr, R. G., Amin, K., O'Neill, M. E., & Britton, B. G. (1988). Dosage effects and individual responsivity to methylphenidate in attention deficit disorder. *Journal of Child Psychology and Psychiatry, 29*, 453-475.

Douglas, V. I., & Parry, P. A. (1983). Effects of reward on delayed reaction time task performance of hyperactive children. *Journal of Abnormal Child Psychology, 11*, 313-326.

DuPaul, G. J., Rapport, M. D., & Perriello, L. M. (1991). Teacher ratings of academic skills: The development of the Academic Performance Rating Scale. *School Psychology Review, 20*, 284-300.

Elia, J., Borcherding, B. G., Rapoport, J. L., & Keysor, C. S. (1991). Methylphenidate and dextroamphetamine treatments of hyperactivity: Are there true nonresponders? *Psychiatry Research, 36*, 141-155.

Engel, G. L. (1977). The need for a new medical model: A challenge to medicine. *Science, 196*, 129-136.

Erhardt, D., & Hinshaw, S. P. (1993). *Initial sociometric impressions of hyperactive and comparison boys: Predictions from behavioral and nonbehavioral variables.* Manuscript submitted for publication.

Eysenck, H. J. (1986). A critique of classification and diagnosis. In T. Millon & G. Klerman (Eds.), *Contemporary directions in psychopathology: Toward the DSM-IV* (pp. 73-98). New York: Guilford.

Faraone, S., Biederman, J., Chen, W. J., Krifcher, B., Keenan, K., Moore, C., Sprich, S., & Tsuang, M. T. (1992). Segregation analysis of attention-deficit hyperactivity disorder: Evidence for single gene transmission. *Psychiatric Genetics, 2*, 257-276.

Faraone, S. V., Biederman, J., Keenan, K., & Tsuang, M. T. (1991a). A family-genetic study of girls with DSM-III attention deficit disorder. *American Journal of Psychiatry, 148*, 112-117.

Faraone, S. V., Biederman, J., Krifcher, B., Keenan, K., Moore, C., Ugaglia, K., Jellinek, M. S., Spencer, T., Norman, D., Seidman, L., Kolodny, R., Benjamin, J., Kraus, I., Perrin, J., Chen, W., & Tsuang, M. T. (1992). Evidence for independent trasmission in families for Attention Deficit Hyperactivity Disorder (ADHD) and learning disability: Results from a family genetic study of ADHD. *American Journal of Psychiatry, 150,* 891-895.

Faraone, S. V., Biederman, J., Lehman, B. K. Spencer, T., Norman, D., Seidman, L. J., Kraus, I., Perrin, J., Chen, W. J., & Tsuang, M. T. (in press). Intellectual performance and school failure in children with attention deficit hyperactivity disorder and in their siblings. *Journal of Abnormal Psychology.*

Farrington, D. M., Loeber, R., & Van Kammen, W. B. (1990). Long-term criminal outcomes of hyperactivity-impulsivity-attention deficit and conduct problems in childhood. In L. N. Robins & M. Rutter (Eds.), *Straight and devious pathways from childhood to adulthood* (pp. 62-81). Cambridge, UK: Cambridge University Press.

Fergusson, D. M., Horwood, L. J., & Lloyd, M. (1991). Confirmatory factor models of attention deficit and conduct disorder. *Journal of Child Psychology and Psychiatry, 32,* 257-274.

Fergusson, D. M., Horwood, L. J., & Lynskey, M. T. (1993). Early dentine lead levels and subsequent cognitive and behavioural development. *Journal of Child Psychology and Psychiatry, 34,* 215-227.

Firestone, P. (1982). Factors associated with children's adherence to stimulant medication. *American Journal of Orthopsychiatry, 52,* 447-457.

Fischer, M., Barkley, R. A., Edelbrock, C. S., & Smallish, L. (1990). The adolescent outcome of hyperactive children diagnosed by research criteria: II. Academic, attentional, and neuropsychological status. *Journal of Consulting and Clinical Psychology, 58,* 580-588.

Fischer, M., Barkley, R. A., Fletcher, K. E., & Smallish, L. (1993). The adolescent outcome of hyperactive children: Predictors of psychiatric, academic, social, and emotional adjustment. *Journal of the American Academy of Child and Adolescent Psychiatry, 32,* 324-332.

Fisher, P., Shaffer, D., Piacentini, J., Lapkin, J., Wicks, J., & Rojas, M. (1991). *Completion of revisions of the NIMH Diagnostic Interview Schedule for Children (DISC-2).* Washington, DC: Epidemiology and Psychopathology Research, National Institute for Mental Research.

Fitzpatrick, P. A., Klorman, R., Brumaghim, J. T., & Borgstedt, A. D. (1992). Effects of sustained-release and standard preparations of methylphenidate on attention deficit disorder. *Journal of the American Academy of Child and Adolescent Psychiatry, 31,* 226-234.

Frick, P. J., Kamphaus, R. W., Lahey, B. B., Loeber, R., Christ, M. A. G., Hart, E. S., & Tannenbaum, L. E. (1991). Academic underachievement and the disruptive behavior disorders. *Journal of Consulting and Clinical Psychology, 59,* 289-294.

Frick, P. J., Lahey, B. B., Loeber, R., Stouthamer-Loeber, M., Christ, M.A.G., & Hanson, K. (1992). Familial risk factors to oppositional defiant disorder and conduct disorder: Parental psychopathology and maternal parenting. *Journal of Consulting and Clinical Psychology, 60,* 49-55.

Gadow, K. D. (1992). Pediatric psychopharmacotherapy: A review of recent research. *Journal of Child Psychology and Psychiatry, 33,* 153-195.

Gadow, K. D., Nolan, E. E., Sverd, J., Sprafkin, J., & Paolicelli, L. (1990). Methylphenidate in aggressive-hyperactive boys: I. Effects on peer aggression in public school settings. *Journal of the American Academy of Child and Adolescent Psychiatry, 29,* 710-718.

Gandour, M. J. (1989). Activity level as a dimension of temperament in toddlers: Its relevance for the organismic specificity hypothesis. *Child Development, 60*, 1092-1098.

Garmezy, N. (1989). Stress-resistant children: The search for protective factors. In J. E. Stevenson (Ed.), *Aspects of current child psychiatry research* (pp. 213-233). Oxford, UK: Pergamon.

Gittelman, R., Abikoff, H., Pollack, E., Klein, D. F., Katz, S., & Mattes, J. (1980). A controlled trial of behavior modification and methylphenidate in hyperactive children. In C. K. Whalen & B. Henker (Eds.), *Hyperactive children: The social ecology of identification and treatment* (pp. 221-243). New York: Academic Press.

Gittelman, R., & Feingold, I. (1983). Children with reading disorders—I. Efficacy of reading remediation. *Journal of Child Psychology and Psychiatry, 24*, 167-191.

Gittelman, R., Klein, D. F., & Feingold, I. (1983). Children with reading disorders: II. Effects of methylphenidate in combination with reading remediation. *Journal of Child Psychology and Psychiatry, 24*, 193-212.

Gittelman, R., Mannuzza, S., Shenker, R., & Bonagura, N. (1985). Hyperactive boys almost grown up. *Archives of General Psychiatry, 42*, 937-947.

Goodman, R., & Stevenson, J. (1989a). A twin study of hyperactivity—I. An examination of hyperactivity scores and categories derived from Rutter parent and teacher questionnaires. *Journal of Child Psychology and Psychiatry, 30*, 671-689.

Goodman, R., & Stevenson, J. (1989b). A twin study of hyperactivity—II. The aetiological role of genes, family relationships, and perinatal adversity. *Journal of Child Psychology and Psychiatry, 30*, 691-709.

Goodwin, F., & Jamison, K. R. (1990). *Manic-depressive illness.* New York: Oxford University Press.

Goodyear, P., & Hynd, G. W. (1992). Attention-deficit disorder with (ADD/H) and without (ADD/WO) hyperactivity: Behavioral and neuropsychological differentiation. *Journal of Clinical Child Psychology, 21*, 273-305.

Goyette, C. H., Conners, C. K., & Ulrich, R. F. (1978). Normative data on Revised Conners Parent and Teacher Rating Scales. *Journal of Abnormal Child Psychology, 6*, 221-236.

Gray, J. A. (1982). *The neuropsychology of anxiety.* New York: Oxford University Press.

Greenhill, L. L., & Osman, B. P. (1991). *Ritalin: Theory and patient management.* New York: Liebert.

Haenlein, M., & Caul, W. F. (1987). Attention deficit disorder with hyperactivity: A specific hypothesis of reward dysfunction. *Journal of the American Academy of Child and Adolescent Psychiatry, 26*, 356-362.

Halperin, J. M., Gittelman, R., Klein, D. F., & Rudel, R. G. (1984). Reading-disabled hyperactive children: A distinct subgroup of attention deficit disorder with hyperactivity? *Journal of Abnormal Child Psychology, 12*, 1-14.

Halperin, J. M., Matier, K., Bedi, G., Sharma, V., & Newcorn, J. H. (1992). Specificity of inattention, impulsivity, and hyperactivity to the diagnosis of attention-deficit hyperactivity disorder. *Journal of the American Academy of Child and Adolescent Psychiatry, 31*, 190-196.

Halperin, J. M., Wolf, L., Greenblatt, E. R., & Young, G. (1991). Subtype analysis of commission errors on the continuous performance test in children. *Developmental Neuropsychology, 7*, 207-217.

Halperin, J. M., Wolf, L. E., Pascualvaca, D. M., Newcorn, J. H., Healey, J. M., O'Brien, J. D., Morganstern, A., & Young, J. G. (1988). Differential assessment of attention and impulsivity in children. *Journal of the American Academy of Child and Adolescent Psychiatry, 27*, 326-329.

Hart, E. L., Applegate, B., Lahey, B. B., Loeber, R., Hynd, G. W., Horn, K., & Green, S. (1993). *The factor structure of attention deficit disorder and implications for DSM-IV*. Manuscript submitted for publication.

Hauser, P., Zametkin, A. J., Martinez, P., Vitiello, B., Matochik, J. A., Mixson, A. J., & Weintraub, B. D. (1993). Attention deficit-hyperactivity disorder in people with generalized resistance to thyroid hormone. *New England Journal of Medicine, 328*, 997-1001.

Herjanic, B., Herjanic, M., Brown, F., & Wheatt, T. (1975). Are children reliable reporters? *Journal of Abnormal Child Psychology, 3*, 41-48.

Hetherington, E. M., & Martin, B. (1986). Family interaction patterns. In H. C. Quay & J. S. Werry (Eds.), *Psychopathological disorders of childhood* (3rd. ed., pp. 349-408). New York: John Wiley.

Hinshaw, S. P. (1987a). Hyperactivity, attention deficit disorders, and learning disabilities. In V. B. Van Hasselt & M. Hersen (Eds.), *Psychological evaluation of the developmentally and physically disabled* (pp. 213-260). New York: Plenum.

Hinshaw, S. P. (1987b). On the distinction between attentional deficits/hyperactivity and conduct problems/aggression in child psychopathology. *Psychological Bulletin, 101*, 443-463.

Hinshaw, S. P. (1991). Stimulant medication and the treatment of aggression in children with attentional deficits. *Journal of Clinical Child Psychology, 20*, 301-312.

Hinshaw, S. P. (1992a). Academic underachievement, attentional deficits, and aggression: Comorbidity and implications for intervention. *Journal of Consulting and Clinical Psychology, 60*, 893-903.

Hinshaw, S. P. (1992b). Externalizing behavior problems and academic underachievement in childhood and adolescence: Causal relationships and underlying mechanisms. *Psychological Bulletin, 111*, 127-155.

Hinshaw, S. P. (1992c). Intervention for social skill and social competence. *Child and Adolescent Psychiatric Clinics of North America, 1*, 539-552.

Hinshaw, S. P. (in press). Conduct disorder in childhood: Conceptualization, diagnosis, comorbidity, and risk status for antisocial functioning in adulthood. In D. Fowles, P. Sutker, & S. Goodman (Eds.), *Psychopathy and antisocial personality: A developmental perspective*. New York: Springer.

Hinshaw, S. P., Buhrmester, D., & Heller, T. (1989). Anger control in response to verbal provocation: Effects of stimulant medication for boys with ADHD. *Journal of Abnormal Child Psychology, 17*, 393-407.

Hinshaw, S. P., & Erhardt, D. (1991). Attention-deficit hyperactivity disorder. In P. C. Kendall (Ed.), *Child and adolescent therapy: Cognitive-behavioral procedures* (pp. 98-128). New York: Guilford.

Hinshaw, S. P., & Erhardt, D. (1993). Behavioral treatment. In V. B. Van Hasselt & M. Hersen (Eds.), *Handbook of behavior therapy and pharmacotherapy for children: A comparative analysis* (pp. 233-250). Needham Heights, MA: Allyn & Bacon.

Hinshaw, S. P., Han, S. S., Erhardt, D., & Huber, A. (1992). Internalizing and externalizing behavior problems in preschool children: Correspondence among parent and teacher ratings and behavior observations. *Journal of Clinical Child Psychology, 21*, 143-150.

Hinshaw, S. P., Heller, T., & McHale, J. P. (1992). Covert antisocial behavior in boys with attention-deficit hyperactivity disorder: External validation and effects of methylphenidate. *Journal of Consulting and Clinical Psychology, 60*, 274-281.

Hinshaw, S. P., Henker, B., & Whalen, C. K. (1984a). Cognitive-behavioral and pharmacologic interventions for hyperactive boys: Comparative and combined effects. *Journal of Consulting and Clinical Psychology, 52*, 739-749.

Hinshaw, S. P., Henker, B., & Whalen, C. K. (1984b). Self-control in hyperactive boys in anger-inducing situations: Effects of cognitive-behavioral training and of methylphenidate. *Journal of Abnormal Child Psychology, 12*, 55-77.

Hinshaw, S. P., Henker, B., Whalen, C. K., Erhardt, D., & Dunnington, R. E. (1989). Aggressive, prosocial, and nonsocial behavior in hyperactive boys: Dose effects of methylphenidate in naturalistic settings. *Journal of Consulting and Clinical Psychology, 57*, 636-643.

Hinshaw, S. P., Lahey, B. B., & Hart, E. L. (1993). Issues of taxonomy and comorbidity in the development of conduct disorder. *Development and Psychopathology, 5*, 31-49.

Hinshaw, S. P., & Nigg, J. (in press). Behavioral rating scales in the assessment of disruptive dehavior disorders in childhood. In D. Shaffer & J. Richters (Eds.), *Assessment in child psychopathology*. New York: Plenum.

Hodges, K. (1993). Structured interviews for assessing children. *Journal of Child Psychology and Psychiatry, 34*, 49-68.

Hodges, K., Kline, J., Stern, L., Cytryn, L., & McKnew, D. (1982). The development of a child assessment interview for research and clinical use. *Journal of Abnormal Child Psychology, 10*, 173-189.

Huesmann, L. D., & Eron, L. R. (1990). The stability of aggressive behavior—even unto the third generation. In M. Lewis & S. M. Miller (Eds.), *Handbook of developmental psychopathology* (pp. 146-156). New York: Plenum.

Huesmann, L. D., Eron, L. R., Lefkowitz, M. M., & Walder, L. O. (1984). Stability of aggression over time and generations. *Developmental Psychology, 20*, 1120-1134.

Hynd, G. W., Hern, K. L., Voeller, K. K., & Marshall, R. M. (1991). Neurobiological basis of attention-deficit hyperactivity disorder (ADHD). *School Psychology Review, 20*, 174-186.

Jacobvitz, D., & Sroufe, L. A. (1987). The early caregiver-mother relationship and attention deficit disorder with hyperactivity in kindergarten: A prospective study. *Child Development, 58*, 1488-1495.

James, A., & Taylor, E. (1990). Sex differences in the hyperkinetic syndrome of childhood. *Journal of Child Psychology and Psychiatry, 31*, 437-446.

Kaufman, A. S., & Kaufman, N. L. (1983). *Kaufman Assessment Battery for Children*. Circle Pines, MN: American Guidance Service.

Kavale, K., & Forness, S. (1983). Hyperactivity and diet treatment: A meta-analysis of the Feingold hypothesis. *Journal of Learning Disabilities, 16*, 324-330.

Kazdin, A. E. (1987). Treatment of antisocial behavior in children: Current status and future directions. *Psychological Bulletin, 102*, 187-203.

Kazdin, A. E., Bass, D., Siegel, T., & Thomas, C. (1989). Cognitive-behavioral therapy and relationship therapy in the treatment of children referred for antisocial behavior. *Journal of Consulting and Clinical Psychology, 57*, 522-535.

Klein, R. G., & Mannuzza, S. (1991). Long-term outcome of hyperactive children: A review. *Journal of the American Academy of Child and Adolescent Psychiatry, 30*, 383-387.

Klorman, R., Brumaghim, J. T., Salsman, L. F., Strauss, J., Borgstedt, A. D., McBride, M. C., & Loeb, S. (1988). Effects of methylphenidate on attention deficit hyperactivity disorder with and without aggressive/noncompliant features. *Journal of Abnormal Psychology, 97*, 413-422.

Kramer, J. (1993, February). Childhood hyperactivity and aggression as differential predictors of adolescent progression to alcoholism vs. drug abuse. In J. Loney (Chair), *External validation of child hyperactivity and aggression.* Symposium conducted at the annual meeting of the Society for Research on Child and Adolescent Psychopathology, Santa Fe, NM.

Kupietz, S. S., Winsberg, B. G., Richardson, E., Maitinsky, S., & Mendell, N. (1988). Effects of methylphenidate dosage in hyperactive-reading disabled children: I. Behavior and cognitive performance. *Journal of the American Academy of Child and Adolescent Psychiatry, 27*, 70-77.

Lahey, B. B. (1993, February). *Update on the DSM-IV diagnostic criteria for attention-deficit hyperactivity disorder.* Paper presented at the annual meeting of the Professional Group for Attention-Deficit and Related Disorders, Santa Fe.

Lahey, B. B., & Carlson, C. L. (1991). Validity of the diagnostic category of attention deficit disorder without hyperactivity: A review of the literature. *Journal of Learning Disabilities, 24*, 110-120.

Lahey, B. B., Hartdagen, S. E., Frick, P. J., McBurnett, K., Connor, R., & Hynd, G. W. (1988). Conduct disorder: Parsing the confounded relationship between parental divorce and antisocial personality. *Journal of Abnormal Psychology, 97*, 163-170.

Lahey, B. B., Pelham, W. E., Schaughency, E. A., Atkins, M. S., Murphy, H. A., Hynd, G. W., Russo, M., Hartdagen, S., & Lorys-Vernon, A. (1988). Dimensions and types of attention deficit disorder with hyperactivity in children: A factor and cluster analytic approach. *Journal of the American Academy of Child and Adolescent Psychiatry, 27*, 330-335.

Lahey, B. B., Piacentini, J. C., McBurnett, K., Stone, P., Hartdagen, S., & Hynd, G. W. (1988). Psychopathology in the parents of children with conduct disorder and hyperactivity. *Journal of the American Academy of Child and Adolescent Psychiatry, 27*, 163-170.

Lahey, B. B., Schaughency, E. A., Hynd, G. W., Carlson, C. L., & Nieves, N. (1987). Attention deficit disorder with and without hyperactivity: Comparison of behavioral characteristics of clinic-referred children. *Journal of the American Academy of Child and Adolescent Psychiatry, 26*, 718-723.

Landau, S., & Milich, R. (1988). Social communication patterns of attention-deficit-disordered boys. *Journal of Abnormal Child Psychology, 16*, 69-81.

Laufer, M. W., & Denhoff, E. (1957). Hyperkinetic behavior syndrome in children. *Journal of Pediatrics, 50*, 463-473.

Lewis, M. (1990). Models of developmental psychopathology. In M. Lewis & S. M. Miller (Eds.), *Handbook of developmental psychopathology* (pp. 15-27). New York: Plenum.

Lilienfeld, S. O., & Waldman, I. D. (1990). The relationship between childhood attention-deficit hyperactivity disorder and adult antisocial behavior re-examined: The problem of heterogeneity. *Clinical Psychology Review, 10*, 699-725.

Loeber, R. (1982). The stability of antisocial and delinquent child behavior: A review. *Child Development, 53*, 1431-1446.

Loeber, R., Green, S. M., Lahey, B. B., & Stouthamer-Loeber, M. (1991). Differences and similarities between children, mothers, and teachers as informants on disruptive behavior disorders. *Journal of Abnormal Child Psychology, 19*, 75-95.

Loeber, R., Lahey, B. B., & Thomas, C. (1991). Diagnostic conundrum of oppositional defiant disorder and conduct disorder. *Journal of Abnormal Psychology, 100*, 379-390.

Loeber, R., & Schmaling, K. B. (1985). Empirical evidence for overt and covert patterns of antisocial conduct problems: A meta-analysis. *Journal of Abnormal Child Psychology, 13*, 337-352.

Loney, J. (1987). Hyperactivity and aggression in the diagnosis of attention deficit disorder. In B. B. Lahey & A. E. Kazdin (Eds.), *Advances in clinical child psychology* (Vol. 10, pp. 99-135). New York: Plenum.

Loney, J., Kramer, J., & Milich, R. (1981). The hyperactive child grows up: Predictors of symptoms, delinquency, and achievement at follow-up. In K. D. Gadow & J. Loney (Eds.), *Psychosocial aspects of drug treatment for hyperactivity* (pp. 381-415). Boulder, CO: Westview.

Loney, J., & Milich, R. (1982). Hyperactivity, inattention, and aggression in clinical practice. In M. Wolraich & D. K. Routh (Eds.), *Advances in developmental and behavioral pediatrics* (Vol. 2, pp. 113-147). Greenwich, CT: JAI.

Loney, J., Whaley-Klahn, M. A., Kosier, T., & Conboy, J. (1983). Hyperactive boys and their brothers at 21: Predictors of aggressive and antisocial outcomes. In K. T. van Dusen & S. A. Mednick (Eds.), *Prospective studies of crime and delinquency* (pp. 181-206). Boston: Kluwer-Nijhoff.

Lou, H. C., Henriksen, L., & Bruhn, P. (1984). Focal cerebral hypoperfusion in children with dysphasia and/or attention deficit disorder. *Archives of Neurology, 41*, 825-829.

Luria, A. R. (1966). *Higher cortical functions in man.* New York: Basic Books.

Magnusson, D. (1987). Adult delinquency in the light of conduct and physiology at an early age: A longitudinal study. In D. Magnusson & A. Ohman (Eds.), *Psychopathology: An interactional perspective* (pp. 221-234). Orlando, FL: Academic Press.

Mannuzza, S., & Gittelman, R. (1984). The adolescent outcome of hyperactive girls. *Psychiatry Research, 13*, 19-29.

Mannuzza, S., Gittelman, R. G., Konig, P. H., & Giampino, T. L. (1990). Childhood predictors of psychiatric status in the young adulthood of hyperactive boys: A study controlling for chance associations. In L. N. Robins & M. Rutter (Eds.), *Straight and devious pathways from childhood to adulthood* (pp. 279-299). Cambridge, UK: Cambridge University Press.

Mannuzza, S., Klein, R. G., & Addalli, K. A. (1991). Young adult mental status of hyperactive boys and their brothers: A prospective follow-up study. *Journal of the American Academy of Child and Adolescent Psychiatry, 30*, 743-751.

Mannuzza, S., Klein, R. G., Bonagura, N., Malloy, P., Giampino, T. L., & Addalli, K. A. (1991). Hyperactive boys almost grown up: V. Replication of psychiatric status. *Archives of General Psychiatry, 48*, 77-83.

Mash, E. J., & Johnston, C. (1990). Determinants of parenting stress: Illustrations from families of hyperactive children and families of physically abused children. *Journal of Clinical Child Psychology, 19*, 313-338.

Mash, E. J., & Terdal, L. G. (1988). Behavioral assessment of child and family disturbance. In E. J. Mash & L. G. Terdal (Eds.), *Behavioral assessment of childhood disorders* (2nd ed., pp. 3-69). New York: Guilford.

Maughan, B., Gray, G., & Rutter, M. (1985). Reading retardation and antisocial behavior: A follow-up into employment. *Journal of Child Psychology and Psychiatry, 26*, 741-758.

Maziade, M., Cote, R., Bernier, H., Boutin, P., & Thivierge, J. (1989). Significance of extreme temperament in infancy for clinical status in pre-school years. I: Value of extreme temperament at 4-8 months for predicting diagnosis at 4.7 years. *British Journal of Psychiatry, 154*, 535-543.

McBurnett, K. (1992). Psychobiological approaches to personality and their applications to child psychopathology. In B. B. Lahey & A. E. Kazdin (Eds.), *Advances in clinical child psychology* (pp. 107-164). New York: Plenum.

McConaughy, S. H., Achenbach, T. M., & Kent, C. L. (1988). Multiaxial empirically based assessment: Parent, teacher, observational, cognitive, and personality correlates of child behavior profiles in 6- to 11-year-old boys. *Journal of Abnormal Child Psychology, 16*, 485-509.

McCracken, J. T. (1991). A two-part model of stimulant action on attention-deficit hyperactivity disorder in children. *Journal of Neuropsychiatry, 3*, 201-209.

McGee, R., & Feehan, M. (1991). Are girls with problems of attention underrecognized? *Journal of Psychopathology and Behavioral Assessment, 13*, 187-198.

McGee, R., Stanton, W. R., & Sears, M. R. (1993). Allergic disorders and attention deficit disorder in children. *Journal of Abnormal Child Psychology, 21*, 79-88.

McGee, R., Williams, S. M., & Silva, P. A. (1987). A comparison of girls and boys with teacher-identified problems of attention. *Journal of the American Academy of Child and Adolescent Psychiatry, 26*, 711-717.

Mednick, S. A., Brennan, P., & Kandel, E. (1988). Predisposition to violence. *Aggressive Behavior, 14*, 25-33.

Meehl, P. E., & Golden, R. R. (1982). Taxometric methods. In P. C. Kendall & J. N. Butcher (Eds.), *Handbook of research methods in clinical psychology* (pp. 127-181). New York: John Wiley.

Meichenbaum, D. H. (1977). *Cognitive-behavior modification: An integrative approach.* New York: Plenum.

Melnick, S., & Hinshaw, S. P. (1993, March). *What do hyperactive children want? Subgroup differences in goals for a social interaction.* Poster presented at the biennial meeting of the Society for Research in Child Development, New Orleans, LA.

Milich, R., Carlson, C. L., Pelham, W. E., & Licht, B. G. (1991). Effects of methylphenidate on the persistence of ADHD boys following failure experiences. *Journal of Abnormal Child Psychology, 19*, 266-282.

Milich, R., & Dodge, K. A. (1984). Social information processing in child psychiatry populations. *Journal of Abnormal Child Psychology, 12*, 471-489.

Milich, R., Hartung, C., Martin, C., & Haigler, E. (1993, February). Disinhibition and underlying processes in hyperactive and aggressive adolescents. In J. Loney (Chair), *External validation of child hyperactivity and aggression.* Symposium conducted at the annual meeting of the Society for Research in Child and Adolescent Psychopathology, Santa Fe.

Milich, R., & Kramer, J. (1984). Reflections on impulsivity: An empirical investigation of impulsivity as a construct. In K. Gadow & I. Bialer (Eds.), *Advances in learning and behavioral disabilities* (Vol. 3, pp. 57-94). Greenwich, CT: JAI.

Milich, R., & Landau, S. (1982). Socialization and peer relations in hyperactive children. In K. D. Gadow & I. Bialer (Eds.), *Advances in learning and behavioral disabilities* (Vol 1., pp. 283-339). Greenwich, CT: JAI.

Milich, R., & Landau, S. (1989). The role of social status variables in differentiating subgroups of hyperactive children. In L. M. Bloomingdale & J. M. Swanson (Eds.), *Attention deficit disorder* (Vol. 4, pp. 1-16). Oxford: Pergamon.

Milich, R., & Loney, J. (1979). The role of hyperactive and aggressive symptomatology in predicting adolescent outcome among hyperactive children. *Journal of Pediatric Psychology, 4*, 93-112.

Milich, R., Widiger, T., & Landau, S. (1987). Differential diagnosis of attention deficit and conduct disorders using conditional probabilities. *Journal of Consulting and Clinical Psychology, 55*, 762-767.

Milich, R., Wolraich, M. C., & Lindgren, S. (1986). Sugar and hyperactivity: A critical review of empirical findings. *Clinical Psychology Review, 6*, 493-513.

Moffitt, T. E. (1990). Juvenile delinquency and attention deficit disorder: Boys' developmental trajectories from age 3 to 15. *Child Development, 61*, 893-910.

Moffitt, T. E. (1993). The neuropsychology of conduct disorder. *Development and Psychopathology, 5*, 135-151.

Moffitt, T. E. (in press). "Life-course-persistent" and "adolescence-limited" antisocial behavior: A developmental taxonomy. *Psychological Review.*

Moffitt, T. E., & Silva, P. A. (1988). Self-reported delinquency, neuropsychological assessment, and history of attention deficit disorder. *Journal of Abnormal Child Psychology, 16*, 553-569.

Needleman, H. L., Schell, A., Bellinger, D. C., Leviton, L., & Allred, E. D. (1990). The long-term effects of exposure to low doses of lead in childhood: An 11-year follow-up report. *New England Journal of Medicine, 322*, 83-88.

Newcomb, A. F., Bukowski, W. M., & Pattee, L. (1993). Children's peer relations: A meta-analytic review of popular, rejected, neglected, controversial, and average sociometric status. *Psychological Bulletin, 113*, 99-128.

Nichols, P. L., & Chen, T. (1981). *Minimal brain dysfunction: A prospective study.* Hillsdale, NJ: Lawrence Erlbaum.

O'Daugherty, M., Nuechterlein, K., & Drew, B. (1984). Hyperactive and hypoxic children: Signal detection, sustained attention, and behavior. *Journal of Abnormal Psychology, 93*, 178-191.

Ohman, A., & Magnusson, D. (1987). An interactional paradigm for research on psychopathology. In D. Magnusson & A. Ohman (Eds.), *Psychopathology: An interactional perspective* (pp. 3-21). Orlando, FL: Academic Press.

O'Leary, K. D. (1980). Pills or skills for hyperactive children? *Journal of Applied Behavior Analysis, 13*, 191-204.

Parker, J. G., & Asher, S. R. (1987). Peer relations and later personal adjustment: Are low-accepted children at risk? *Psychological Bulletin, 102*, 357-389.

Paternite, C. E., & Loney, J. (1980). Childhood hyperkinesis: Relationships between symptomatology and home environment. In C. K. Whalen & B. Henker (Eds.), *Hyperactive children: The social ecology of identification and treatment* (pp. 105-141). New York: Academic Press.

Patterson, G. R. (1982). *Coercive family process.* Eugene, OR: Castalia.

Pelham, W. E. (1986). The effects of stimulant drugs on learning and achievement in hyperactive and learning-disabled children. In J. K. Torgesen & B. Wong (Eds.),

Psychological and educational perspectives on learning disabilities (pp. 259-295). Orlando, FL: Academic Press.

Pelham, W. E., & Bender, M. E. (1982). Peer relationships in hyperactive children: Description and treatment. In K. Gadow & I. Bialer (Eds.), *Advances in learning and behavioral disabilities* (Vol. 1, pp. 365-436). Greenwich, CT: JAI.

Pelham, W. E., Bender, M. E., Caddell, J., Booth, S., & Moorer, S. K. (1985). Methylphenidate and children with attention deficit disorder: Dose effects on classroom academic and social behavior. *Archives of General Psychiatry, 42*, 948-952.

Pelham, W. E., Carlson, C., Sams, S. E., Vallano, G., Dixon, M. J., & Hoza, B. (1993). Separate and combined effects of methylphenidate and behavior modification on the classroom behavior and academic performance of ADHD boys: Group effects and individual differences. *Journal of Consulting and Clinical Psychology, 61*, 506-515.

Pelham, W. E., Gnagy, E. M., Greenslade, K. E., & Milich, R. (1992). Teacher ratings of DSM-III-R symptoms for the disruptive behavior disorders. *Journal of the American Academy of Child and Adolescent Psychiatry, 31*, 210-218.

Pelham, W. E., & Hinshaw, S. P. (1992). Behavioral intervention for ADHD. In S. M. Turner, K. S. Calhoun, & H. E. Adams (Eds.), *Handbook of clinical behavior therapy* (2nd ed., pp. 259-283). New York: John Wiley.

Pelham, W. E., & Milich, R. (1991). Measuring ADHD children's response to psychostimulant medication: Prediction and individual differences. In L. L. Greenhill & B. P. Osman (Eds.), *Ritalin: Theory and patient management* (pp. 203-221). New York: Liebert.

Pelham, W. E., Milich, J., & Walker, J. L. (1987). Effects of continuous and partial reinforcement and methylphenidate on learning in children with attention deficit disorder. *Journal of Abnormal Psychology, 93*, 319-325.

Pelham, W. E., Murphy, D. A., Vannatta, K., Milich, R., Licht, B. G., Gnagy, E. M., Greenslade, K. E., Greiner, A. R., & Vodde-Hamilton, M. (1992). Methylphenidate and attributions in boys with attention-deficit hyperactivity disorder. *Journal of Consulting and Clinical Psychology, 60*, 282-292.

Pelham, W. E., & Murphy, H. A. (1986). Behavioral and pharmacological treatment of attention deficit and conduct disorders. In M. Hersen (Ed.), *Pharmacological and behavioral treatment: An integrative approach* (pp. 108-148). New York: John Wiley.

Pelham, W. E., Schnedler, R., Bologna, N., & Contreras, A. (1980). Behavioral and stimulant treatment of hyperactive children: A therapy study with methylphenidate probes in a within-subject design. *Journal of Applied Behavior Analysis, 13*, 221-236.

Pelham, W. E., Vodde-Hamilton, M., Murphy, D. A., Greenstein, J., & Vallano, G. (1991). The effects of methylphenidate on ADHD adolescents in recreational, peer group, and classroom settings. *Journal of Clinical Child Psychology, 20*, 301-312.

Pelham, W. E., Walker, J. L., Sturges, J., & Hoza, J. (1989). Comparative effects of methylphenidate on ADD girls and ADD boys. *Journal of the American Academy of Child and Adolescent Psychiatry, 28*, 773-776.

Piacentini, J. C., Cohen, P., & Cohen, J. (1992). Combining discrepant information from multiple sources: Are complex algorithms better than simple ones? *Journal of Abnormal Child Psychology, 20*, 51-63.

Pisterman, S., McGrath, P., Firestone, P., Goodman, J. T., Webster, I., & Mallory, R. (1989). Outcome of parent-mediated treatment of preschoolers with ADDH. *Journal of Consulting and Clinical Psychology, 57*, 628-635.

Pliszka, S. R. (1987). Tricyclic antidepressants in the treatment of attention deficit disorder. *Journal of the American Academy of Child and Adolescent Psychiatry, 26,* 127-132.

Pliszka, S. R. (1989). Effect of anxiety on cognition, behavior, and stimulant response in ADHD. *Journal of the American Academy of Child and Adolescent Psychiatry, 28,* 882-887.

Plomin, R. (1986). *Development, genetics, and psychology.* Hillsdale, NJ: Lawrence Erlbaum.

Plomin, R., Nitz, K., & Rowe, D. C. (1990). Behavioral genetics and aggressive behavior in childhood. In M. Lewis & S. M. Miller (Eds.), *Handbook of developmental psychopathology* (pp. 119-133). New York: Plenum.

Porrino, L. J., Rapoport, J. L., Behar, D., Sceery, W., Ismond, D. R., & Bunney, W. E. (1983). A naturalistic assessment of the motor activity of hyperactive boys: I. Comparison with normal controls. *Archives of General Psychiatry, 40,* 681-687.

Prendergast, M., Taylor, E., Rapoport, J. L., Bartko, J., Donnelly, M., Zametkin, A., Ahearn, M. B., Dunn, G., & Wieselberg, H. M. (1988). The diagnosis of childhood hyperactivity: A U.S.-U.K. cross-national study of DSM-III and ICD-9. *Journal of Child Psychology and Psychiatry, 29,* 289-300.

Price, J. M., & Dodge, K. A. (1989). Reactive and proactive aggression in childhood: Relations to peer status and social context dimensions. *Journal of Abnormal Child Psychology, 17,* 455-471.

Psychopharmacology Bulletin (1985). Special issue on measures in child psychopharmacology research, *21,* No. 3.

Puig-Antich, J., & Chambers, W. (1978). *The Schedule for Affective Disorders and Schizophrenia for School-age Children (Kiddie-SADS).* New York: New York State Psychiatric Institute.

Quay, H. C. (1979). Classification. In H. C. Quay & J. S. Werry (Eds.), *Psychopathological disorders of childhood* (2nd ed., pp. 1-42). New York: John Wiley.

Quay, H. C. (1988). The behavioral reward and inhibition systems in childhood behavior disorder. In L. M. Bloomingdale (Ed.), *Attention deficit disorder* (Vol. 3, pp. 176-186). New York: Pergamon.

Quay, H. C., & Peterson, D. R. (1983). *Interim manual for the Revised Behavior Problem Checklist* (1st ed.). Unpublished manuscript, University of Miami.

Rapoport, J. L., Buchsbaum, M. S., Zahn, T., Weingartner, H., Ludlow, C., & Mikkelsen, E. J. (1978). Dextroamphetamine: Cognitive and behavioural effects in normal prepubertal boys. *Science, 199,* 560-563.

Rapport, M. D., DuPaul, G. J., & Denny, C. (1993, February). *Methylphenidate effects on behavior and academic functioning in children with ADDH: An empirical examination of dosage effects, outcome probabilities, and normalization rates in 76 children.* Paper presented at the annual meeting of the Society for Research on Child and Adolescent Psychopathology, Santa Fe.

Rapport, M. D., Murphy, H. A., & Bailey, J. S. (1982). Ritalin vs. response cost in the control of hyperactive children: A within-subject comparison. *Journal of Applied Behavior Analysis, 15,* 205-216.

Rapport, M. D., Stoner, G., DuPaul, G. J., Kelly, K. L., Tucker, S. B., & Schoeler, T. (1988). Attention deficit disorder and methylphenidate: A multilevel analysis of dose-response effects on children's impulsivity across settings. *Journal of the American Academy of Child and Adolescent Psychiatry, 27,* 60-69.

Richman, N., Stevenson, J., & Graham, P. J. (1982). *Preschool to school: A behavioural study.* New York: Academic Press.

Richters, J. E., & Cicchetti, D. (1993). Mark Twain meets DSM-III-R: Conduct disorder, development, and the concept of harmful dysfunction. *Development and Psychopathology, 5,* 5-29.

Richters, J., Jensen, P. S., Arnold, L. E., Abikoff, H., Conners, C. K., Greenhill, L. L., Hechtman, L. T., Hinshaw, S. P., Pelham, W. E., & Swanson, J. M. (1993). *NIMH Collaborative Multisite, Multimodality Intervention Study of ADHD/ADD.* Unpublished manuscript, National Institute of Mental Health.

Rie, H. E., & Rie, E. D. (Eds.). (1980). *Handbook of minimal brain dysfunctions: A critical view.* New York: John Wiley.

Roberts, M. A. (1990). A behavioral observation method for differentiating hyperactive and aggressive boys. *Journal of Abnormal Child Psychology, 18,* 131-142.

Roberts, M. A. (1993, February). Predictors of adult psychiatric diagnoses in hyperactive boys: Child hyperactivity and aggression, parent psychopathology, and parenting style. In J. Loney (Ed.), *External validation of child hyperactivity and aggression.* Symposium conducted at the annual meeting of the Society for Research in Child and Adolescent Psychopathology, Santa Fe.

Robins, L. N., & McEvoy, L. (1990). Conduct problems as predictors of substance abuse. In L. N. Robins & M. Rutter (Eds.), *Straight and devious pathways from childhood to adulthood* (pp. 182-204). Cambridge, UK: Cambridge University Press.

Robins, L. N., & Regier, D. A. (Eds.). (1991). *Psychiatric disorders in America: The Epidemiological Catchment Area study.* New York: The Free Press.

Robinson, P. W., Newby, T. J., & Ganzell, S. L. (1981). A token system for a class of underachieving children. *Journal of Applied Behavior Analysis, 14,* 307-315.

Rodin, J., Elias, M., Silberstein, L. R., & Wagner, A. (1988). Combined behavioral and pharmacologic treatment for obesity: Predictors of successful weight maintenance. *Journal of Consulting and Clinical Psychology, 56,* 399-404.

Rosen, L. A., O'Leary, S. G., Joyce, S. A., Conway, G., & Pfiffner, L. J. (1984). The importance of prudent negative consequences for maintaining the appropriate behavior of hyperactive students. *Journal of Abnormal Child Psychology, 12,* 581-604.

Ross, D. M., & Ross, S. A. (1982). *Hyperactivity: Current issues, research, and theory.* New York: John Wiley.

Rutter, M. (1982). Syndromes attributed to "minimal brain dysfunction" in childhood. *American Journal of Psychiatry, 139,* 21-33.

Rutter, M. (1983). Behavioral studies: Questions and findings on the concept of a distinctive syndrome. In M. Rutter (Ed.), *Developmental neuropsychiatry* (pp. 259-279). New York: Guilford.

Rutter, M. (1989). Pathways from childhood to adult life. *Journal of Child Psychology and Psychiatry, 30,* 23-51.

Rutter, M., Bolton, P., Harrington, R., LeCouteur, A., Macdonald, H., & Simonoff, E. (1990a). Genetic factors in child psychiatric disorders—I. A review of research strategies. *Journal of Child Psychology and Psychiatry, 31,* 3-37.

Rutter, M., Macdonald, H., LeCouteur, A., Harrington, R., Bolton, P., & Bailey, A. (1990b). Genetic factors in child psychiatric disorders—II. Empirical findings. *Journal of Child Psychology and Psychiatry, 31,* 39-83.

Rutter, M., & Yule, W. (1975). The concept of specific reading retardation. *Journal of Child Psychology and Psychiatry, 16,* 181-197.

Safer, D. J., & Krager, J. M. (1988). A survey of medication treatment for hyperactive/in-attentive students. *Journal of the American Medical Association, 260*, 2256-2258.

Sandoval, J., Lambert, N. M., & Sassone, D. (1980). The identification and labeling of hyperactivity in children: An interactive model. In C. K. Whalen & B. Henker (Eds.), *Hyperactive children: The social ecology of identification and treatment* (pp. 145-171). New York: Academic Press.

Satterfield, J. H., Cantwell, D. P., & Satterfield, B. T. (1979). Multimodality treatment: A one-year follow-up of 84 hyperactive boys. *Archives of General Psychiatry, 36*, 965-974.

Satterfield, J. H., Hoppe, C. M., & Schell, A. M. (1982). A prospective study of delin-quency in 110 adolescent boys with attention deficit disorder and 88 normal adolescent boys. *American Journal of Psychiatry, 139*, 795-798.

Satterfield, J. H., Satterfield, B. T., & Cantwell, D. P. (1981). Three-year multimodality treatment study of 100 hyperactive boys. *Journal of Pediatrics, 98*, 650-655.

Satterfield, J. H., Satterfield, B. T., & Schell, A. M. (1987). Therapeutic interventions to prevent delinquency in hyperactive boys. *Journal of the American Academy of Child and Adolescent Psychiatry, 26*, 56-64.

Schachar, R. (1986). Hyperkinetic syndrome: Historical development of the concept. In E. A. Taylor (Ed.), *The overactive child* (pp. 19-40). London: MacKeith.

Schachar, R. (1991). Childhood hyperactivity. *Journal of Child Psychology and Psychiatry, 32*, 155-191.

Schachar, R., Logan, G., Wachsmuth, R., & Chajczyk, D. (1988). Attaining and maintain-ing preparation: A comparison of attention in hyperactive, normal, and disturbed control children. *Journal of Abnormal Child Psychology, 16*, 361-378.

Schachar, R., Rutter, M., & Smith, A. (1981). The characteristics of situationally and pervasively hyperactive children: Implications for syndrome definition. *Journal of Child Psychology and Psychiatry, 22*, 375-392.

Schachar, R., Sandberg, S., & Rutter, M. (1986). Agreement between teachers' ratings and observations of hyperactivity, inattentiveness, and defiance. *Journal of Abnormal Child Psychology, 14*, 331-345.

Schachar, R., & Wachsmuth, R. (1990). Hyperactivity and parental psychopathology. *Journal of Child Psychology and Psychiatry, 31*, 381-392.

Seidel, W. T., & Joschko, M. (1990). Evidence of difficulties in sustained attention in children with ADDH. *Journal of Abnormal Child Psychology, 18*, 217-229.

Semrud-Clikeman, M., Biederman, J., Sprich-Buckminster, S., Lehman, B. K., Faraone, S. V., & Norman, D. (1992). Comorbidity between ADDH and learning disability: A review and report in a clinically referred sample. *Journal of the American Academy of Child and Adolescent Psychiatry, 31*, 439-448.

Sergeant, J., & Scholten, C. A. (1985). On resource strategy limitations in hyperactivity: Cognitive impulsivity reconsidered. *Journal of Child Psychology and Psychiatry, 26*, 97-109.

Shelton, T., & Barkley, R. A. (1990). Clinical, developmental, and biopsychosocial considerations. In R. A. Barkley, *Attention-deficit hyperactivity disorder: A hand-book for diagnosis and treatment* (pp. 209-231). New York: Guilford.

Simmel, C., & Hinshaw, S. P. (1993, March). *Moral reasoning and antisocial behavior in boys with ADHD.* Poster presented at the biennial meeting of the Society for Research in Child Development, New Orleans.

Sleator, E. K., & Ullmann, R. K. (1981). Can the physician diagnose hyperactivity in the doctor's office? *Pediatrics, 67,* 13-17.

Sprague, R. L., & Sleator, E. K. (1977). Methylphenidate in hyperkinetic children: Differences in dose effects on learning and social behavior. *Science, 198,* 1274-1276.

Spreen, O. (1988). Prognosis of learning disability. *Journal of Consulting and Clinical Psychology, 56,* 836-842.

Sroufe, L. A. (1979). The coherence of individual development. *American Psychologist, 34,* 834-841.

Sroufe, L. A., & Rutter, M. (1984). The domain of developmental psychopathology. *Child Development, 55,* 17-24.

Stevenson, J. (1992). Evidence for a genetic etiology of hyperactivity in children. *Behavior Genetics, 22,* 337-343.

Still, G. F. (1902). Some abnormal psychical conditions in children. *Lancet, 1,* 1077-1082.

Strauss, A. A., & Lehtinen, L. E. (1947). *Psychopathology and education of the brain-injured child.* New York: Grune & Stratton.

Sullivan, M. A., & O'Leary, S. G. (1989). Differential maintenance following reward and cost token programs with children. *Behavior Therapy, 21,* 139-151.

Swanson, J. M. (1992). *School-based assessments and interventions for ADD students.* Irvine, CA: K. C. Publishing.

Swanson, J. M., Cantwell, D., Lerner, M., McBurnett, K., & Hanna, G. (1991). Effects of stimulant medication on learning in children with ADHD. *Journal of Learning Disabilities, 24,* 219-230.

Szatmari, P., Boyle, M., & Offord, D. R. (1989). ADDH and conduct disorder: Degree of diagnostic overlap and differences among correlates. *Journal of the American Academy of Child and Adolescent Psychiatry, 28,* 865-872.

Szatmari, P., Offord, D. R., & Boyle, M. H. (1989). Ontario Child Health Study: Prevalence of attention deficit disorder with hyperactivity. *Journal of Child Psychology and Psychiatry, 30,* 219-230.

Taylor, E., Schachar, R., Thorley, G., Wieselberg, H. M., Everitt, B., & Rutter, M. (1987). Which boys respond to stimulant medication? A controlled trial of methylphenidate in boys with disruptive behavior. *Psychological Medicine, 17,* 121-143.

Thorley, G. (1984). Review of follow-up and follow-back studies of childhood hyperactivity. *Psychological Bulletin, 96,* 116-132.

Uhlenhuth, E. H., Lipman, R. S., & Covi, L. (1969). Combined pharmacotherapy and psychotherapy: Controlled studies. *Journal of Nervous and Mental Disease, 148,* 52-64.

Ullmann, R. K., Sleator, E. K., & Sprague, R. L. (1985). A change of mind: The Conners Abbreviated Rating Scales reconsidered. *Journal of Abnormal Child Psychology, 13,* 553-565.

van der Meere, J., van Baal, M., & Sergeant, J. (1989). The additive factor method: A differential diagnostic tool in hyperactivity and learning disability. *Journal of Abnormal Child Psychology, 17,* 409-422.

van der Meere, J., Wekking, E., & Sergeant, J. (1991). Sustained attention and pervasive hyperactivity. *Journal of Child Psychology and Psychiatry, 32,* 275-284.

Voeller, K.K.S. (1991). What can neurological models of attention, intention, and arousal tell us about attention-deficit hyperactivity disorder? *Journal of Neuropsychiatry, 3,* 209-216.

Wakefield, J. C. (1992). The concept of mental disorder: On the boundary between biological facts and social values. *American Psychologist, 47*, 373-388.

Walker, J. L., Lahey, B. B., Hynd, G. W., & Frame, C. L. (1987). Comparison of specific patterns of antisocial behavior in children with conduct disorder with or without coexisting hyperactivity. *Journal of Consulting and Clinical Psychology, 55*, 910-913.

Wechsler, D. (1991). *Wechsler Intelligence Scale for Children* (3rd ed.). New York: The Psychological Corporation.

Wechsler, D. (1992). *Wechsler Individual Achievement Test*. New York: The Psychological Corporation.

Weiss, G., & Hechtman, L. (1986). *Hyperactive children grown up: Empirical findings and theoretical considerations*. New York: Guilford.

Wender, P. H., Reimherr, F. W., Wood, D., & Ward, M. (1985). A controlled study of methylphenidate in the treatment of attention deficit disorder, residual type, in adults. *American Journal of Psychiatry, 142*, 547-552.

Werner, E., & Smith, S. (1977). *Kauai's children come of age*. Honolulu: University of Hawaii Press.

Werry, J. S., Elkind, G. S., & Reeves, J. C. (1987). Attention deficit, conduct, oppositional, and anxiety disorders in children: III. Laboratory differences. *Journal of Abnormal Child Psychology, 15*, 409-428.

Whalen, C. K. (1989). Attention-deficit hyperactivity disorder. In T. H. Ollendick & M. Hersen (Eds.), *Handbook of child psychopathology* (2nd ed., pp. 131-169). New York: Plenum.

Whalen, C. K., & Henker, B. (1976). Psychostimulants and children: A review and analysis. *Psychological Bulletin, 83*, 1113-1130.

Whalen, C. K., & Henker, B. (1980). *Hyperactive children: The social ecology of identification and treatment*. New York: Academic Press.

Whalen, C. K., & Henker, B. (1985). The social worlds of hyperactive (ADDH) children. *Clinical Psychology Review, 5*, 447-478.

Whalen, C. K., & Henker, B. (1991). Therapies for hyperactive children: Comparisons, combinations, and compromises. *Journal of Consulting and Clinical Psychology, 59*, 126-137.

Whalen, C. K., & Henker, B. (1992). The social profile of attention-deficit hyperactivity disorder: Five fundamental facets. *Child and Adolescent Psychiatric Clinics of North America, 1*, 395-410.

Whalen, C. K., Henker, B., Buhrmester, D., Hinshaw, S. P., Huber, A., & Laski, K. (1989). Does stimulant medication improve the peer status of hyperactive children? *Journal of Consulting and Clinical Psychology, 57*, 545-549.

Whalen, C. K., Henker, B., Collins, B. E., McAuliffe, S., & Vaux, A. (1979). Peer interaction in a structured communication task: Comparisons of normal and hyperactive boys and of methylphenidate (Ritalin) and placebo effects. *Child Development, 50*, 388-401.

White, J. L., Moffitt, T. E., Caspi, A., Jeglum, D., Needles, D., & Stouthamer-Loeber, M. (in press). Measuring impulsivity and examining its relation to delinquency. *Journal of Abnormal Psychology*.

Wilson, M. (1993). DSM-III and the transformation of American psychiatry: A history. *American Journal of Psychiatry, 150*, 399-410.

Woodcock, R. W., & Johnson, M. B. (1989-1990). *Woodcock-Johnson Psychoeducational Battery-Revised*. Allen, TX: DLM Teaching Resources.

World Health Organization. (1978). *International classification of diseases* (9th ed.). Geneva, Switzerland: World Health Organization.

Zametkin, A. J., Nordahl, T. E., Gross, M., King, A. C., Semple, W. E., Rumsey, J., Hamburger, S., & Cohen, R. M. (1990). Cerebral glucose metabolism in adults with hyperactivity of childhood onset. *New England Journal of Medicine, 323,* 1361-1366.

Zametkin, A. J., & Rapoport, J. L. (1987). Neurobiology of attention deficit disorder with hyperactivity: Where have we come in 50 years? *Journal of the American Academy of Child and Adolescent Psychiatry, 26,* 676-686.

Zupan, B. A. (1991). *Aggressive schemata in boys with attention-deficit hyperactivity disorder.* Unpublished doctoral dissertation, University of California, Los Angeles.

INDEX

Abbreviated Symptom Questionnaire, 32
Abikoff, H., 36, 80, 122
Academic performance, 17, 76-77, 85-86
  ADD with/without hyperactivity, 73
  behavioral outcome predictability and,
    96-97
  evaluation of, 37-38
  treatment effects, 108-109, 114
Achenbach, T., 28-29, 40
Acting-out behavior. *See* Antisocial be-
  havior; Externalizing behavior
ADD. *See* Attention deficit disorder
Addalli, K., 86
Additives, 63
ADHD. *See* Attention-deficit hyperac-
  tivity disorders
Adolescence-limited delinquency, 95
Adolescent outcomes, 85-86.
  See also Outcome
Adult outcomes, 86-87. *See also* Outcome
Affective disorders, 78-79
Aggression, 16-17, 74-76, 91-94
  ADD with/without hyperactivity, 71
  behavioral treatments, 117
  cumulative neuropsychopathological
    effects, 90
  familial interactions, 76
  gender and, 80
  measurement, 27
  neurological insult and, 9
  peer rejection and, 18, 55, 75
  stimulant treatment, 107
Alcohol consumption, 62, 92
Allergic reactions, 62-63
Antidepressants, 111

Antisocial behavior:
  ADHD comorbidity, 16-17
  childhood ADHD progression, 85-87
  dimensional versus categorical predic-
    tive factors, 7-8
  early and adolescence-limited onset,
    95
  familial interactions, 18, 64, 98
  genetic predisposition, 60
  predictors for, 91-94
  stimulant treatment, 107
  underachievement and, 96-97
  See also Aggression
Anxiety disorders, 77-79, 87
Appetite, 110
Assessment, 22-24, 38-39, 44
  achievement-related functioning, 37-
    38
  behavior observations, 25, 26, 36-37
  causal factor interactions, 29-30
  child self-report, 23, 28, 34-35, 40, 41-
    42
  competencies, 39
  continuous (dimensional) versus
    categorical classifications, 7-8
  cross-informant consistency, 28-29
  defined, 4
  developmental considerations, 30-31,
    94
  field versus clinical situations, 22-23
  integration of multi-source informa-
    tion, 39-40
  interobserver consistency, 25, 26
  interviews, 25, 26, 34-36
  neuropsychological instruments, 38

peer relationships, 38
problems of, 44
rating scales, 32-34
reliability, 25-26
validity, 24, 26-27
Astigraph, 50
Attention, types of, 47
Attentional capacity, 47
Attention deficit disorder (ADD), 70
Attention deficit disorder without hyperactivity, 56, 70-74, 123
Attention-deficit hyperactivity disorders
(ADHD):
alternative models, 51-53
diagnosis. *See* Assessment; Diagnostic
criteria
historical review, 8-11
prevalence, 2, 12, 14-15
prognosis, 1, 2. *See also* Outcome
progression, 18-19. *See also* Outcome
subtypes. *See* Subgroups
symptoms of. *See* Symptoms and
manifestations
treatment. *See* Intervention
Attention deficit. *See* Inattention
Attention deployment tests, 39

Barkley, R., 53-54, 71, 73, 110, 122
Bauermeister, J., 64
Behavioral continuity, 89-90
Behavioral intervention, 112-118
clinical therapy, 115-116, 119
cognitive-behavioral procedures, 113,
116-117
direct contingency management, 114-
115
pharmacologic treatment combina-
tions, 119-122
Behavior models, 3-6, 11. *See also* An-
tisocial behavior; Hyperactivity;
Impulsivity
Behavior observations, 25, 26, 36-37
Behavior Problem Checklist, 33
Bender, M., 54
Benzedrine, 105
Biederman, J., 60, 68, 75, 77
Biomedical model, 3-6

Birth weight, 62
Bonagura, N., 85, 87, 94
Boyle, M., 69, 75
Brain insult, 9
Brain neurochemistry, 61

Cambridge Study for Delinquent
Development, 92
Cantwell, D., 109
Caspi, A., 90
Categorical classifications, 6-8
Causal agents. *See* Etiology; Predictive
factors; Risk factors
Child Behavior Checklist, 33
Child guidance movement, 10
Child self-report, 23, 28, 34-35, 40, 41-42
Church of Scientology, 102
Classifications, 6-8
Classroom Behavior Observation Code,
36
Clements, S., 9
Clinical assessment, 22-23, 37. *See also*
Assessment
Clinical behavior therapy, 115-116, 119
Cocaine, 62
Cognitive-behavioral procedures, 113,
116-117
Cognitive impulsivity, 49
Cohen, J., 40
Cohen, P., 40
Comorbidity, 16-18, 74-79
Computerized attention tasks, 46
Conduct disorder (CD):
ADD with/without hyperactivity, 71
ADHD comorbidity, 16, 74-75
antisocial behavior predictability, 7-8
cumulative neuropsychopathological
effects, 90
of girls, 80
underachievement and, 96-97
Congenital factors, 62
Conners Abbreviated Symptom Question-
naire, 32
Construct validity, 27, 32
Contingency management, 114-115
Continuous behavioral patterns, 89-90
Contracting, 115

Controversial issues, 101-102
Costello, E., 68
Criminality, 86-87, 92-93. *See also* Antisocial behavior; Delinquency
Criterion-related validity, 27
Cross-informant consistency, 28-29
Cross-sectional methodologies, 45
Cross-validation, 98-99
Cumulative behavioral continuity, 90-91
Cutoff scores, 7, 32

Delinquency, 19, 95
    childhood ADHD progression, 85
    comorbid aggression as predictor for, 17
    multimodal treatments and, 121
    peer relations and, 17
    See also Antisocial behavior
Denny, C., 109
Depression, 78-79
Desipramine, 111
Development:
    assessment considerations, 30-31, 94
    continuity, 30-31
    intervention considerations, 117
Developmental psychopathology, 6
Dextroamphetamine, 105, 106
Diagnosis, defined, 4
Diagnostic and Statistical Manual of Mental Disorders, 10-12, 26, 44. *See also specific DSM versions*
Diagnostic criteria, 11-14
    assessment tool reliability and, 26
    cutoff scores, 14, 32
    dimensional versus categorical, 6-8
    historical review, 10-12
    impairment, 12, 15-16
    pervasiveness, 12, 14, 67-69
    preschoolers, 31
    reliability of, 44
    situational symptomatology, 67-69
    stimulant overprescription and, 105-106
    See also Assessment; *specific DSM versions*
Diagnostic Interview Schedule for Children (DISC), 35
Diathesis-stress model, 57

Diet, 63
Dimensional classifications, 6-8
Direct contingency management, 114-115
DISC, 35
Disease model, 3-6
Disinhibition, 9, 50, 51, 54, 56
Doctor's office effect, 23
Dopamine, 61
Douglas, V., 10, 53, 66
DSM-III, 11, 26, 49, 70
DSM-III-R, 11, 26, 33, 35, 50, 68, 70
DSM-IV, 11-14, 26, 35, 56, 69, 70, 82, 105-106
DuPaul, G., 37, 71, 109

Early onset antisocial behavior, 95
Ecological validity, 24
Edelbrock, C., 110
Environmental factors, 22-23, 50, 58, 62-63
Epidemiological Catchment Area study, 8
Epidemiology, diagnostic criteria for, 14
Epinephrine, 61
Equifinality, 11, 65
Etiology, 11-12, 43-44, 57-60
    congenital factors, 62
    environmental agents, 58, 62-63
    family interactions, 58, 61, 63-64
    genetic factors, 60-62
    methodological issues, 44-45
    retrospective versus prospective studies, 58-60
    transactional models, 6
Evaluation. *See* Assessment
Expressive psychotherapy, 112
Externalizing behavior, 4
    familial interactions, 48, 64
    measurement, 33
    rating scales, 25
    underachievement and, 96-97
    See also Antisocial behavior

Factor analytic investigations, 4, 11, 45, 49, 71
Family dysfunction, 18
    ADHD etiology and, 45

ADHD progression and, 86
antisocial behavior and, 93
language deficits and, 97
social class and, 90
Family history, 35
ADD with/without hyperactivity, 71
aggression comorbidity, 75
males and females with ADHD, 79
Family interactions, 58, 61, 63-64, 76
Faraone, S., 75, 77
Farrington, D., 92
Feehan, M., 80-81
Female ADHD, 79-81, 86, 95
Follow-up investigations, 2, 84-87. *See
    also* Outcome
Food additives, 63
Frame, C., 74-75
Frick, P., 96
Frontal lobe function, 52

Gadow, K., 36
Gender differences, 79-81, 86, 95
Genetic factors, 60-62
Girls with ADHD, 79-81, 86, 95
Gittelman, R., 36, 85-86
Glucose metabolism, 61
Goodman, R., 60
Gratification delay, 50
Gray, J., 54

Halperin, J., 48
Hanna, G., 109
Harmful dysfunction, 15-16
Hart, E., 70-71
Hechtman, L., 87, 98, 122
Henker, B., 54
Heritability, 60-62
Heterotypic continuity, 30
Howell, C., 28
Hynd, G., 74-75
Hyperactive-impulsive-attention problem
    (HIA), 92-93
Hyperactive-impulsive subtype, 12
Hyperactivity, 18-19, 50-51
ADHD diagnostic criteria, 11
disinhibitory psychopathology, 54

field versus clinical situations, 22-23
measurement, 7, 38-39, 46, 50
"normal" behavioral patterns, 4
pervasive and situational symptomatol-
    ogy, 67-69
predictors for, 17, 92
subsequent behavioral predictability
    and, 91-93
Hyperkinesis, 32, 33, 67, 80, 82
Hyperkinetic reaction of childhood, 10

Impairment criteria, 12, 15-16
Impulsivity, 49-50
ADHD diagnostic criteria, 11
ADHD symptom clustering, 45-46
familial interactions, 64
measurement, 7, 38-39, 46
"normal" behavioral patterns, 4
Inattention, 47-49
ADHD diagnostic criteria, 11
ADHD symptom clustering, 45-46
measurement, 7, 27, 38-39, 46, 48
"normal" behavioral patterns, 4
stimulant medication response, 105
Inattentive subtype, 12, 56, 70, 82
Infant temperament, 61
Inheritance, 60-62
Intellectual function, 7, 76
antisocial behavior and, 93
family size and, 98
measurement, 37. *See also* IQ
See also Academic performance;
    Learning disabilities
Internal consistency, 25-26
Interobserver consistency, 25, 26
Interpersonal relationships, 54-55. *See
    also* Peer relationships
Intervention:
ADD with/without hyperactivity, 73-74
aggression comorbidity, 75
comorbid psychological/affective dis-
    orders, 78
controversial issues, 101-102
developmental factors and, 117
learning disabilities and, 77
long-term efficacy, 102, 104, 110
maintaining factors, 58

NIMH multimodal trial, 102, 122-123
pharmacologic treatment, 105-112.
  See also Stimulant medications
psychosocial strategies, 112-118. *See
  also* Behavioral interventions
symptom treatment, 103
treatment combinations, 118-122
Interviews, 25, 26, 34-36
IOWA Conners Scale, 33
IQ, 7, 17, 68, 76
  antisocial behavior and, 93
  family size and, 98

Jacobvitz, D., 64

Kaufman Assessment Battery for
    Children, 37
Keenan, K., 75, 77
Klein, D., 36
Klein, R., 69, 85-87, 94
Krager, J., 105
Kramer, J., 49

Lahey, B., 70-71, 74-75
Landau, S., 54, 75
Language deficits, 52, 68, 97
  behavioral treatment effects, 116-117
Lead, 63
Learning disabilities (LD), 17, 76-77
  ADD with/without hyperactivity, 73
  behavior and, 97
  neurological insult and, 9
  See also Academic performance
Lerner, M., 109
Locus coeruleus, 61
Loeber, R., 68, 92
Loney, J., 27, 33, 86, 91-92, 98
Long-term outcome. *See* Outcome
Low birth weight, 62

Magnusson, D., 93
Maintaining factors, 58
Mannuzza, S., 69, 85-87, 94, 98
McBurnett, K., 109

McConaughy, S. H., 28
McGee, R., 80-81
McMurray, M., 71, 110
Medical model, 3-6
Medication response, 73-74, 105, 107-
    110. *See also* Stimulant medications
Memory, 47
Mental disorders, 15-16
Mental retardation, 7
Meta-analytic reviews, 28
Methodological issues, 44-45
Methylphenidate (MPH), 102, 105, 106,
    108, 119. *See also* Stimulant
    medications
Milich, R., 33, 49, 54, 75
Minimal brain dysfunction (MBD), 9, 91
Moffitt, T., 90-91, 93-95
Mood disorders, 78-79, 87
Mother-child interactions, 64
Motivation, 53-54, 76
Motoric overactivity, 50-51
Motor output deficits, 48
MPH (Methylphenidate), 102, 105, 106,
    119
Multivariate statistical models, 7
Murphy, D., 119

National Institute of Mental Health
    (NIMH), 102, 122-123
Neurological function, 9, 52, 62, 90-91
Neuropsychological instruments, 38
Neurotransmitters, 61, 111
Nicotine, 62
NIMH, 102, 122-123
Norepinephrine, 61
Nosology, 5, 12-14, 40

Obesity, 120-121
Offord, D., 69, 75
Operant conditioning, 112
Oppositional-defiant disorder (ODD), 16,
    74, 94
Outcome, 2, 18-19, 84-87, 123
  ADD with/without hyperactivity, 73-
    74
  adolescents, 85-86

aggression comorbidity, 75
behavioral interventions and, 118
behavior observation of, 36
comorbid psychological/affective disorders, 78
continuous and discontinuous patterns, 89-90
medication treatments and, 109-110
predictors of. *See* Predictive factors
psychological disorders, 87
young adults, 86-87
See also specific behaviors
Outcome predictability, 88-91
methodologic issues, 98-99
underachievement and, 96-97
See also Predictive factors

Parent(s):
behavioral therapy programs, 115
mother-child interactions, 64
psychopathology, 18
reliability of as informants, 34-35
See also Family dysfunction
Parenting style, 63-64
Parent Rating Scale, 33
Parry, P., 53
Peer relationships, 17-18, 31, 54-55
ADD with/without hyperactivity, 73
aggressive behavior and, 18, 55, 75
sociometric assessment of, 38
treatment effects, 107-108, 116
Pelham, W., 54, 70-71, 116, 119, 120
Pemoline, 106
Perriello, L., 37
Pervasive symptomatology, 12, 14, 67-69
Pharmacologic intervention, 101-102,
   105-112
aggression comorbidity, 75
alternative agents, 111-112
behavioral treatment combinations,
   119-122
See also Stimulant medications
Piacentini, J., 40
Play therapy, 10
Plomin, R., 60
Predictive factors, 85, 88-91
academic underachievement, 17

aggressive behavior, 17
dimensional versus categorical, 7-8
for antisocial behavior, 91-94
infant temperament, 61
methodologic issues, 98-99
peer rejection, 17-18
underachievement, 96-97
validity of, 98-99
See also Outcome predictability; Risk
   factors
Prevalence, 2
Prognosis, 1, 2. *See also* Outcome
Progression, 18-19, 84-87. *See also* Outcome
continuous and discontinuous patterns,
   89-90
developmental continuity, 30-31
Prospective studies, 59-60, 85, 87, 98
Protective factors, 39
Psychiatric comparison groups, 44-45, 49
Psychodynamic models, 10, 11
Psychological disorders, 77-79, 87
Psychometrics. *See* Rating scales
Psychosocial intervention. *See* Be-
   havioral intervention
Public health, 2

Rapport, M., 37, 109
Rating scales, 25, 32-34
Reading disabilities, 77
Reinforcement, 53, 117
Rejection, 17-18, 38, 55, 75
Reliability, 25-26, 34-35, 44
Remission, 86
Retardation, 7
Retrospective studies, 58-60
Revised Behavior Problem Checklist, 33
Reward-based interventions, 113, 115
Reward sensitivity, 53
Risk factors, 5, 43, 57-58. *See also* Etiol-
   ogy; Predictive factors
familial, 58, 61, 63-64
Ritalin, 102. *See also* Methylphenidate

Safer, D., 105
Satterfield, J., 121

Schachar, R., 68, 80
School dropout, 17
School-related disabilities. *See* Academic
    performance; Peer relationships
Scientology, 102
Selective attention, 47
Self-instructional training, 116-117
Self-regulation, 51-53
Self-report, 23, 28, 34-35, 40, 41-42
Sergeant, J., 47
Serotonin, 61
Short-term memory, 47
Side effects, 110-111
Situational hyperactivity, 68-69
Sleator, E., 108
Sleep disruption, 110
Social class, 90
Social learning models, 11
Social relationships. *See* Peer relationships
Social skills training, 103-104
Sociometric evaluation, 38
Sprague, R., 108
Sroufe, L., 64
Stabilimetric devices, 50
Stevenson, J., 60
Still, G., 9
Stimulant medications, 105-111
    alternative agents, 111-112
    behavioral treatment combinations,
      119-122
    clinical benefits, 107-110
    controversies, 102
    side effects, 110-111
    time course of, 106-107
Stress, 57
Structured interviews, 25, 26, 34-36
Subgroups, 12, 14, 56
    ADD without hyperactivity, 56, 70-74,
      123
    early and adolescence-limited onset, 95
    pervasive and situational symptomatol-
      ogy, 67-69
    See also Comorbidity
Substance abuse, 8, 19, 85, 92
    comorbid aggression as predictor for, 17
    during pregnancy, 62, 66
Sugar, 63
Sustained attention, 47-49

Swanson, J., 109
Symptoms and manifestations:
    clusters, 56
    core dimensions, 45-46
    diagnostic criteria, 11-14
    direct treatment of, 103, 107-109
    field versus clinical situations, 22-23
    minimal brain dysfunction, 9
    pervasive versus situational, 67-69
    remission of, 86
    subsequent behavioral predictability
      and, 91-94
    See also Hyperactivity; Inattention;
      specific symptomatology
Syndromes, 4-5
Szatmari, P., 69, 75

Task completion, 53
Teacher Rating Scale, 33
Teacher training, 115
Teratogenic substances, 62, 66
Thyroid hormone resistance, 57
Tics, 110
Tourette's disorder, 110
Toxins, 58, 62-63
Transactional models, 6, 9
Tricyclic antidepressants, 111
Tsuang, M., 75, 77
Twin studies, 60

Underachievement. *See* Academic perfor-
    mance
Undercontrolled behavior, 4
Undifferentiated ADD, 70

Validity, 24, 26-27, 44
    child's self-report, 34-35
    cross-validation of predictive relation-
      ships, 98-99
Van der Meere, J., 47-48
Van Kammen, W., 92
Verbal mediation deficits, 116-117. *See
    also* Language deficits
Vigilance, 47-49
Vocal tics, 110

Wakefield, J., 15-16
Walker, J., 74-75
Wechsler Individual Achievement Test
  (WIAT), 37
Wechsler Intelligence Scale for Children
  (WISC), 37
Weight control, 120-121
Weiss, G., 87, 98

Werner, E., 62
Whalen, C., 54
Wiggle cushions, 50
Woodcock-Johnson Psychoeducational
  Battery-Revised, 37

Zametkin, A., 61

ABOUT THE AUTHOR

Stephen P. Hinshaw is Associate Professor of Psychology at the University of California, Berkeley. He received his BA from Harvard in 1974 and then directed several treatment programs in New England for children with behavioral and developmental disabilities. After receiving his PhD in Clinical Psychology from the University of California, Los Angeles, in 1983, he performed a postdoctoral fellowship at the University of San Francisco and taught at the University of California, Los Angeles. His research focuses on the development, assessment, and underlying mechanisms of externalizing behavior disorders and on integrated psychosocial-pharmacologic treatment strategies for children with attention deficits and hyperactivity.